IMAGES
of America

HISTORIC
NORTH ST. LOUIS

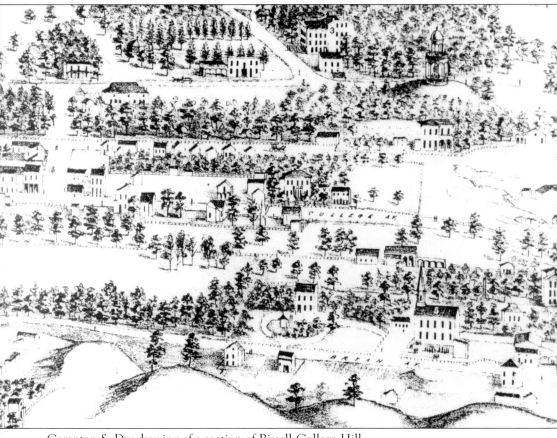

Compton & Dry drawing of a section of Bissell-College Hill.

IMAGES
of America
HISTORIC
NORTH ST. LOUIS

Albert Montesi and Richard Deposki

ARCADIA

Published by Arcadia Publishing,
an imprint of Tempus Publishing, Inc.
3047 N. Lincoln Ave., Suite 410
Chicago, IL 60657

Printed in Great Britain.

Library of Congress Catalog Card Number: 2002117178

For all general information contact Arcadia Publishing at:
Telephone 843-853-2070
Fax 843-853-0044
E-Mail sales@arcadiapublishing.com

For customer service and orders:
Toll-Free 1-888-313-2665

Visit us on the internet at http://www.arcadiapublishing.com

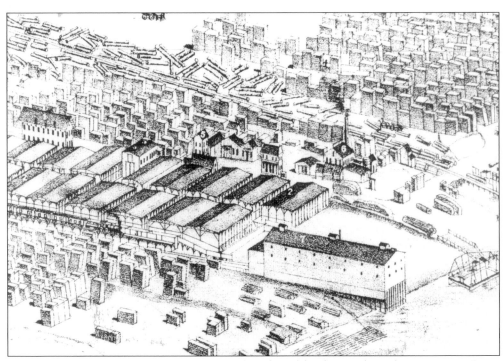

Compton & Dry drawing of the Union Stockyards and lumber yards at the Mississippi River waterfront.

CONTENTS

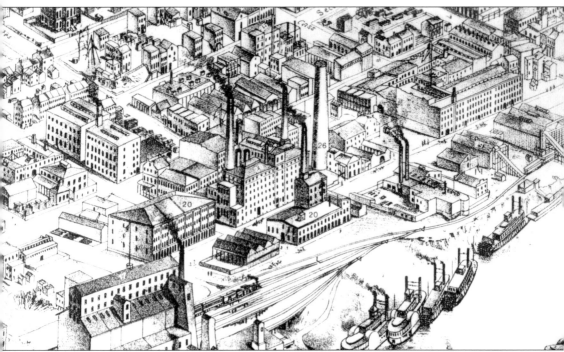

Compton & Dry drawing of Old North St. Louis at the waterfront.

ACKNOWLEDGMENTS

Special thanks to the following for their gracious help in making this book.

Gloria Bratkowski, Tom Bratkowski, Al Hefti, Ron Merzweiler, Edward J. Sokolowski, Piekutowski's European Style Sausage, Diane Roche, Mary Ann Tyra, Steve Marx, Jennifer L Rawlings, Lonnie Tettaton, Bud Schmidt, and Terri Rose. Polish Falcons.
St. Louis University Archives.
Bissell Mansion.
Jane Smith, Tillie Prouder, Jack Prouder.
Metropolitan Sewer District: Frank E. Janson.
Holy Trinity Catholic Church.
Jefferson National Expansion Memorial, NPS.
Old North St. Louis Restoration Group.
Special Collections, St. Louis Public Library.
Westerheide Tobacco and Cigar Company; Ralph Westerheide.
Bremen Bank and Trust Company: Charles W. Nobe, William H. Giese III.
Rev. Richard H.Creason.
Holy Spirit Adoration Sisters.
Tower Village
St. Louis Public Schools Record Center/Archives: Sharon A. Huffman and Gloria Harris.

INTRODUCTION

After St. Louis began to expand in the early 19th century, several communities and villages grew up around it. These were later absorbed by the burgeoning town as the Industrial Revolution and immigration began to reshape the community. Immigrants began settling in record numbers north of the commercial center of town and formed pocket communities of their own. The first settlers in this new land were Anglo-Saxons from New England and other eastern states. They were attracted to the area's profitable trade and came to help build the windmills necessary to produce the goods. The plot of land that this activity encompassed was soon established as a village. And in 1816, it became established as the Village of North St. Louis.

The second wave of ethnic immigrants to the area were Germans, who founded such communities as Bremen and Little Paderhorn, the boundaries of which were determined by their Catholic and Protestant churches and schools. The German Catholics settled around their church at 11th and Biddle Streets, while the German Protestants inhabited the Carr Square area near their Protestant church. Later, when the more prosperous Germans moved out of Carr Square, they were replaced by a new ethnic group, the Jews.

The Irish, suffering from the potato famine, comprised the next immigrant wave and arrived in St. Louis in large numbers. Through the generosity of one Irish family, the Mullanphys, they were allowed to squat on property in Kerry Patch in one-room shacks that they had built for housing. The more affluent Irish later formed communities around the St. Patrick parish at 6th and Biddle Streets.

In 1870, Polish immigrants poured into the Kerry Patch area, supplanting the now mobile Irish who began to move downtown or to the county. The Poles, with their churches and organizations, became one of the most stable and generous populations of North St. Louis to this very day.

Others that came to Near North were Italians not connected to the Italian community on "The Hill." And finally, in the 1920s, immigrants arrived from Russia and the Balkan countries. In 1841, when the Village of North St. Louis had grown in size and population, it was admitted to the city and is known today as Old North St. Louis. Long before this, when the village was first planned, its founders outlined a feature that provided the new neighborhood with distinct character. The planners created three major areas of the town, laid out in three large circles, with each slated to fulfill a need in communal life. The first of these, Jackson Place, was set aside for assembly and recreational purposes; the second, Marion Place, was reserved for a church and cemetery; and the third, Clinton Place, was to be the site of a school. Two of these circles can still be seen today; the third has totally disappeared.

Another segment of this area north of downtown St. Louis was settled by German immigrants in the early 19th century. Calling their neighborhood New Bremen, after a city in northern Germany, these Germans were enticed to settle there through the efforts of Emil Mallinckrodt, the famous chemist. In 1856, Bremen was annexed by the City of St. Louis. Later it became known as Hyde Park.

The last of the neighborhoods that we will feature was originally planned as a community called College Hill, as there were once designs to build a college in its environs. That plan never materialized, however, and the land was turned into subdivisions by developers. It became known as Bissell-College Hill.

In the following pages, we attempt to capture the life and times of these residents as they experienced life in North St. Louis. From this overview of an area that is now in the needed process of renovation and restoration, we see a new day for the North Side of St. Louis. One of the major groups promoting this effort is the Old North St. Louis Restoration Group, whose work in this regard has sparked new interest in reviving the district. They stand firm in doing so despite the political adversaries that sometimes stand in their way.

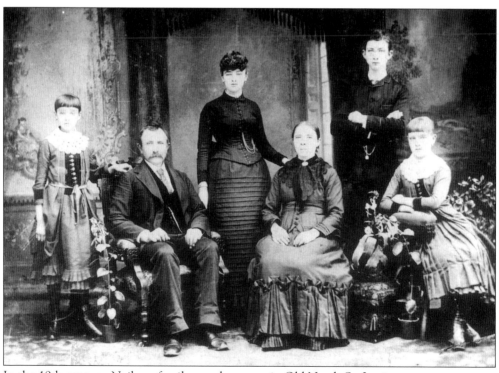

In the 19th century, Neihaus family members pose in Old North St. Louis.

One

BEGINNINGS

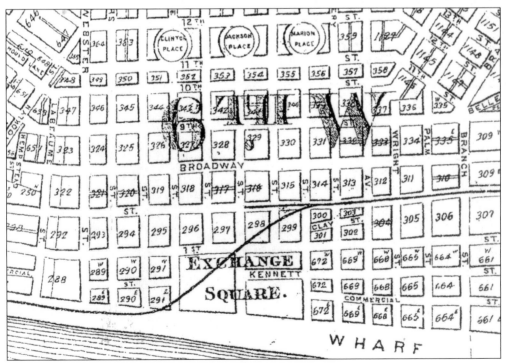

Pictured here is a map of the Village of North St. Louis.

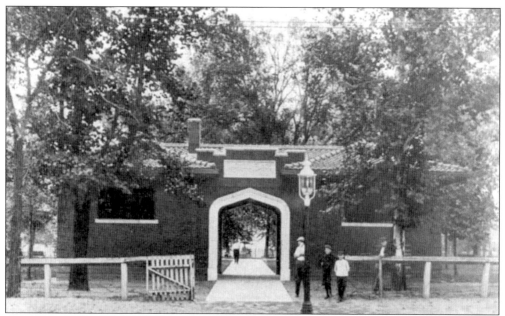

As previously indicated, the early Village of North St. Louis was structured to contain three major circles. Pictured here is the elaborate entrance to Jackson Place, devoted to assembly and recreation. This area of 1.6 acres was the gift of Colonel William Chambers and Major Thomas Wright in 1816. It is located at 11th and N. Market Streets.

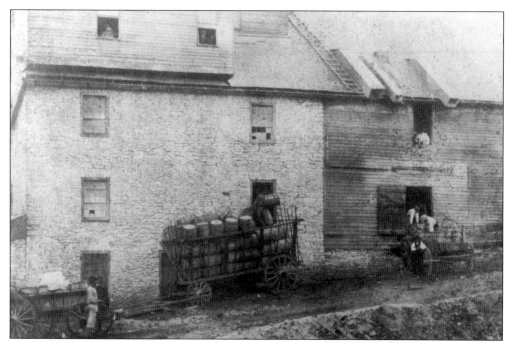

Pictured here is an early steam flour mill constructed in 1819. The first settlers of the village were Anglo-Saxons and hailed from such states as Pennsylvania and Kentucky. They moved west to build the windmills needed to serve the large produce trade emanating from St. Louis at that time. This photograph was taken in 1865.

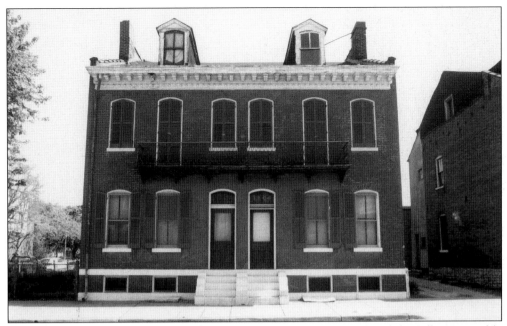

Here is an example of the building design employed by early settlers of the village. Roughly mimicking their Federal and Colonial Eastern antecedents, the homes were generally two to two and a half or three stories high, built close to the sidewalk, and contained one or two dormer windows. Some of these houses were built in the 1830s.

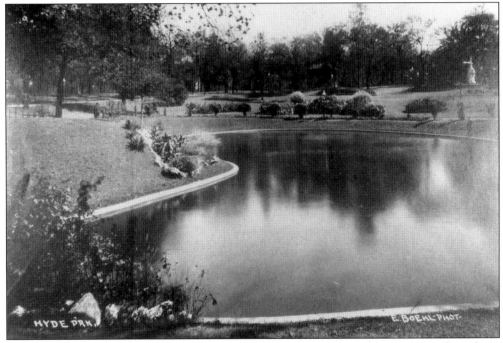

This graceful park was created in 1854 in the Bremen area. It became known as Hyde Park. In July 1863, during the midst of the Civil War, there occurred a violent confrontation of Yankee and Confederate sympathizers that erupted in a riot. Some people were killed.

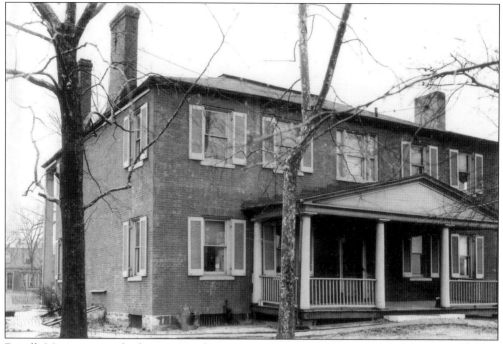

Bissell Mansion was built in 1823 by Captain Lewis Bissell on a bluff overlooking the Mississippi River. (Photo courtesy of Jefferson National Expansion Memorial, NPS.)

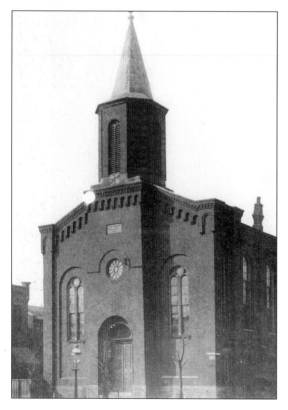

Friedens United Church of Christ, an important architectural gem in North St. Louis, was an elegant structure, whose 80-foot tower was a landmark in the Hyde Park area. It was built in 1860–61 at 19th Street and Newhouse Avenue. It was later demolished for a new building.

Two
NEIGHBORHOODS

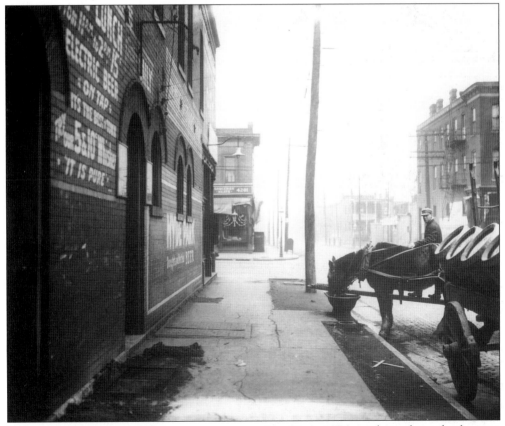

In its heyday, Hyde Park Brewery was very active. From 1876 until its close, the brewery provided much of the area's industry. In this early vintage photo, we can see the Hyde Park Beer ad. (Photo courtesy of Special Collections, St. Louis Public Library.)

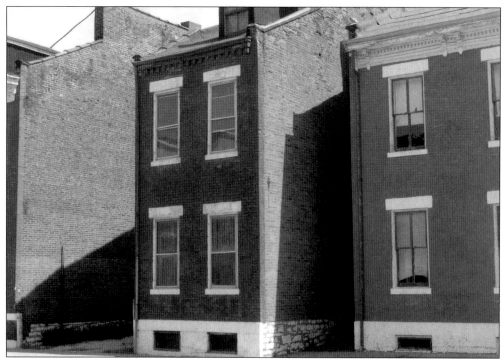

This building, located on Warren Street near 12th Street, is an example of the kind of house designed and built by the earliest settlers in the village of North St. Louis.

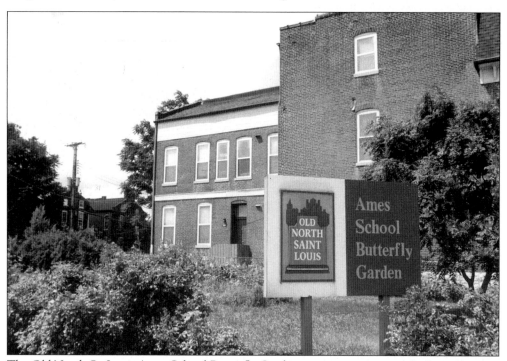

The Old North St. Louis Ames School Butterfly Garden occupies a corner at St. Louis Avenue and 11th Street.

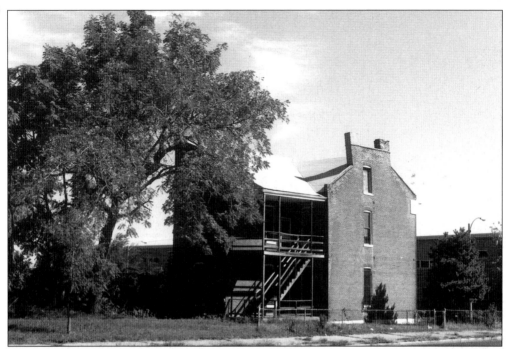

Pictured here is a house at St. Louis and Hadley that retains the long wooden stair to the second floor, an architectural feature most popular with the taste of the day. Notice the pitched roof and the outer wall with few windows. This part of St. Louis Avenue lies close to the center of the original Village of North St. Louis.

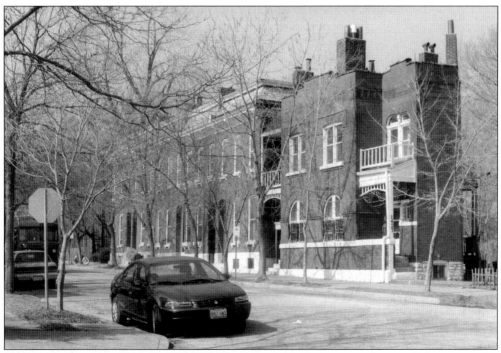

This series of row houses at Blair and Wright Streets is an eclectic rendering of Victorian style.

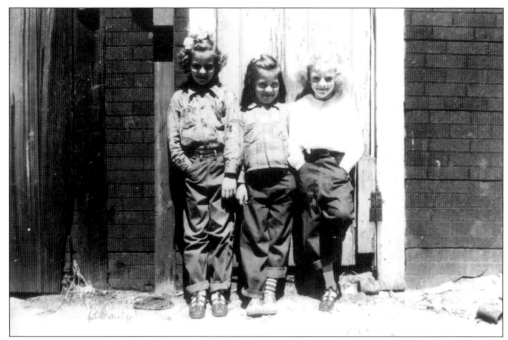

The young folks pictured here lived in North St. Louis during the 1940s. The young ladies, Mary Ann Tyra, right, and two friends, gathered at her home located at 1403 Dodier Street.

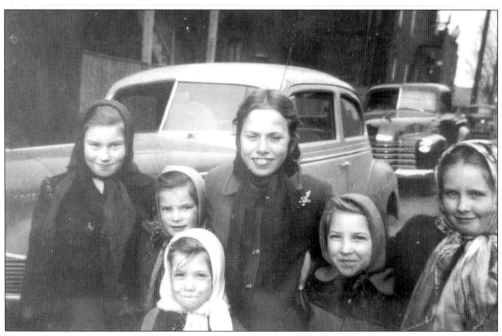

A Sunday school class in 1944–45 poses for a portrait.

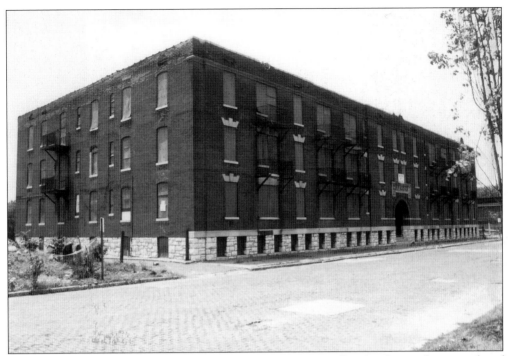

This empty and endangered apartment building at 2118 Mullanphy Street shows marks of neglected beauty. Called the Mullanphy Tenement Building, it was designed by the prestigious Barnett, Haynes, & Barnett firm.

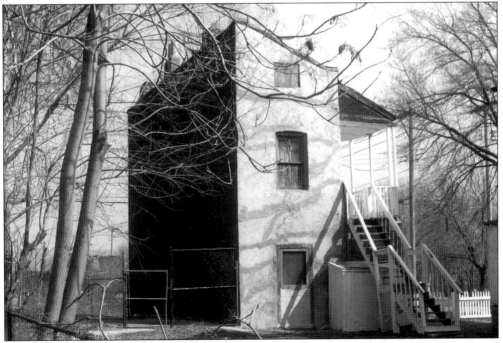

This blockish house was built to resemble a German medieval structure with its flat surfaces and sloping roof. It is often called a flounder style house.

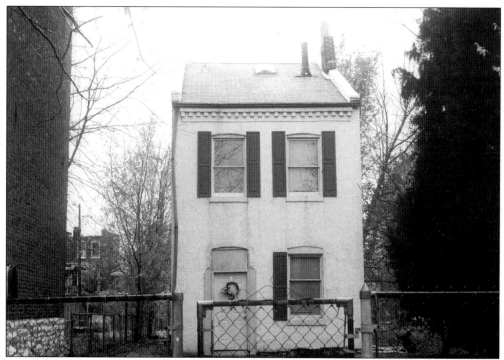

The dentated brick cornice and its shutters give a sense of distinction to this small house at 14th and Hebert Streets.

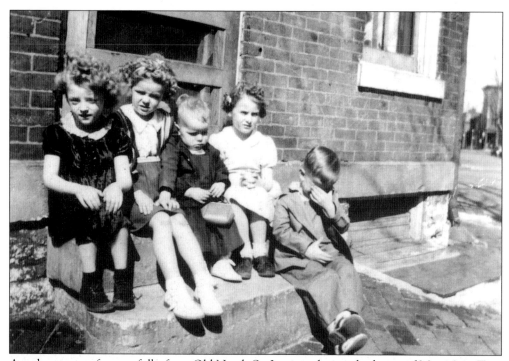

Another group of young folks from Old North St. Louis gather at the home of Mary Ann Tyra in the 1940s.

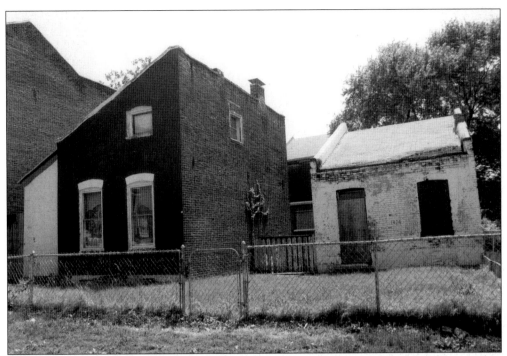

The Hebert Street houses shown here indicate the modest economic reach of some early settlers. While one has a pitched roof, a lean-to porch, and a few windows, it stands next to a more primitive, early German structure that is blockish and small.

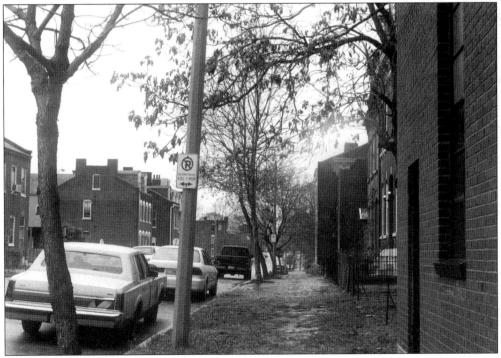

This is the 1400 block of Hebert Street, an area reminiscent of Soulard.

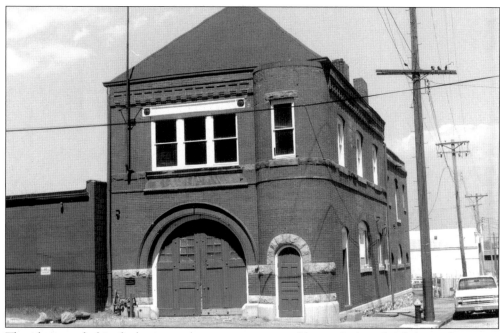

The design of this firehouse and accompanying stable at 2nd and Madison Streets is Richardsonian Romanesque, with its arches and protruding Queen Anne tower. The present owner is converting it to a livable home.

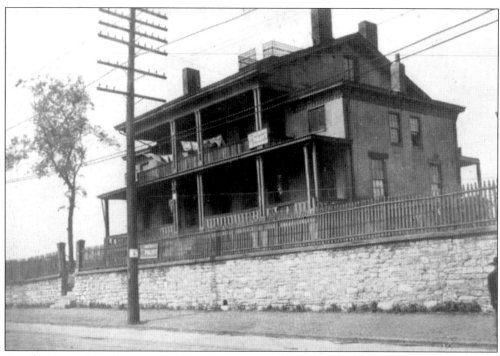

Another impressive home is the Gaty Mansion at 3408 N. 9th Street. Notice the first and second floor verandas, the many windows, and the great size. This is a 1920 photo of a house that has since been demolished.

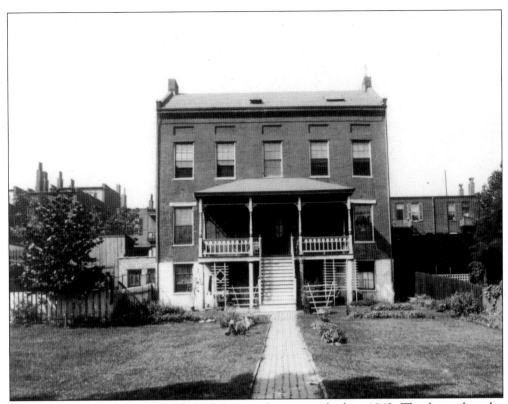

The Adolphus Meier home at 9th and Bremen Streets was built c. 1842. This house has also been demolished.

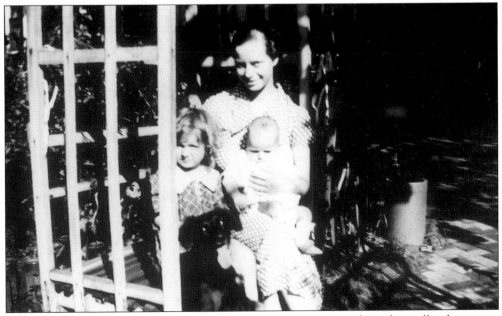

A mother with her baby and a little neighbor pose for the camera from this trellised structure on Grove Street in 1935.

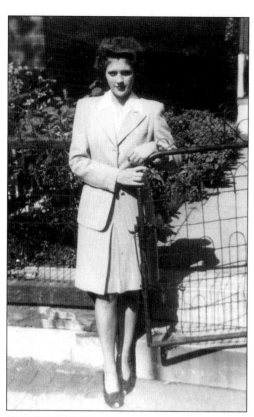

Here again on Grove Street, a well-dressed young lady in the 1940s clutches a wire gate as she poses for her photograph.

Pictured here is one of the Victorian mansions that graced St. Louis Avenue, one of the most prestigious streets in the Near North area where many wealthy families built their homes. In keeping with the modish architecture of the moment, the Second Empire prevailed. The home pictured here follows its Second Empire models rather loosely.

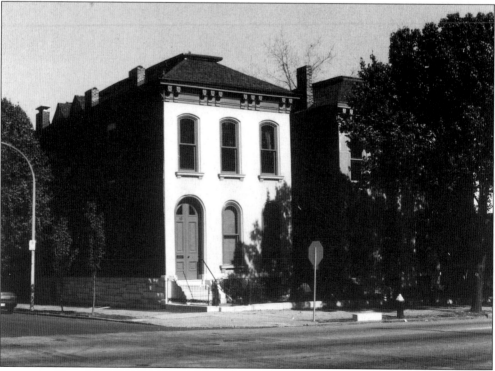

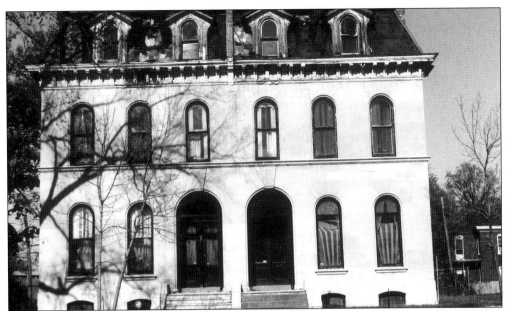

In this example, one can see more clearly some of the Victorian devices that adorned these structures. Notice the mansard roof, dormer windows, decorated cornice, and the arched doors and windows.

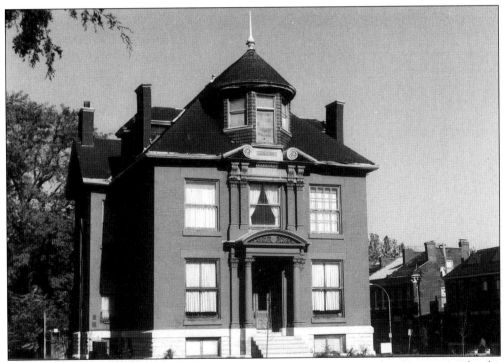

This elegant home on St. Louis Avenue has an imposing portico, made even more so by the continuity of its design. The pitched roof on the second floor and the cubicle variation of the dormer on the third floor emphasize the single upward line. All are variations on Victorian themes and were thought to add majesty to the structure.

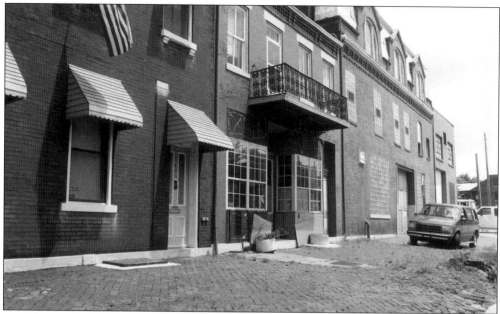

Some of the characteristic architecture of North St. Louis can be also found in some of its modest homes, such as these on N. Market Street. Here a cast iron balcony with multi-paned windows stands next to a house with a sidewalk of brick. The third house boasts three dormer windows. All three, despite their differences, are built in a solid row.

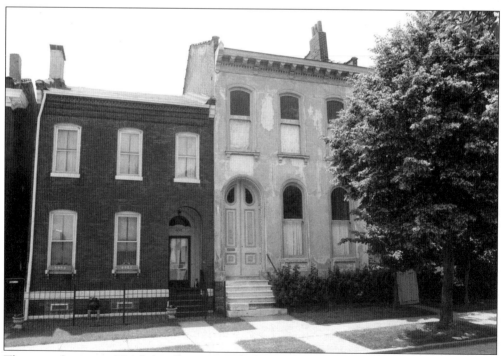

These two homes on N. Market Street provide for yet another study in contrast. The building on the left presents a modest face in contrast to its locked-in neighbor. Notice, however, the arched doorway on both homes.

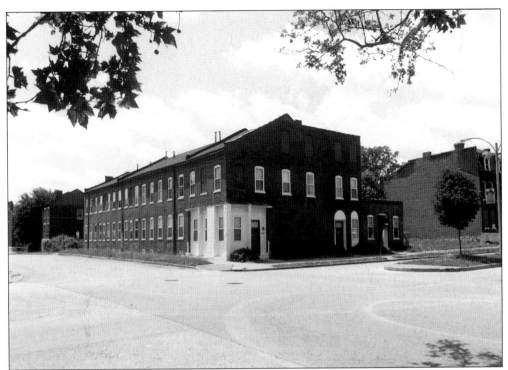

This building on N. Market Street, with its row after row of windows, pitched roof, and flat box-like style, has a stark simplicity of its own. Originally this was a row of domestic dwellings, each with its own entrance and steps.

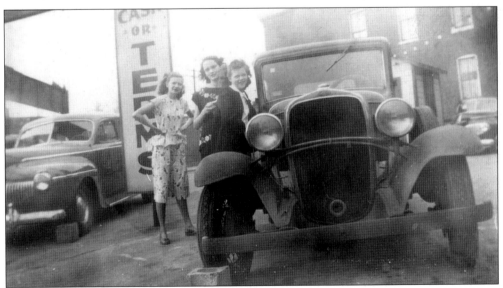

This shot of a used car lot and its prospective buyers was taken in 1946–47.

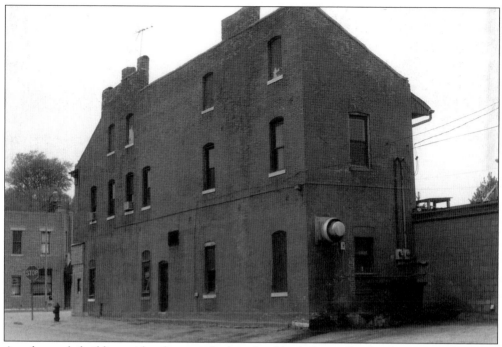

Another early building with a front pitched roof and back flat roof with a business in front can be found at Cornelia Street and Broadway.

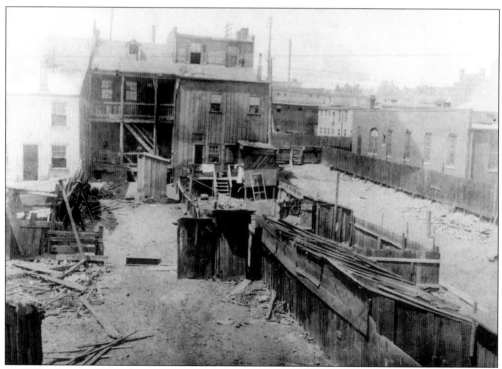

A 1907 picture of the rear of 3216–18 N. Broadway shows a view of a wooden outhouse. A public sewer is available on the street. (Photo courtesy of Metropolitan Sewer District.)

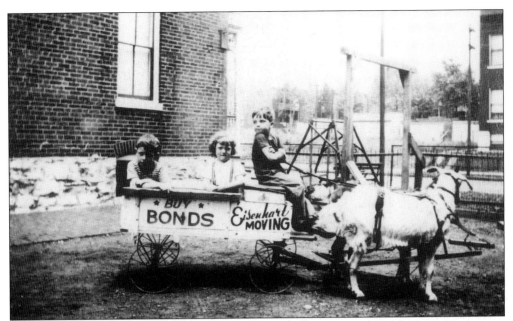
In 1945, Barbara Eisenhart, her brother, and her cousin, rode in a goat-driven wagon.

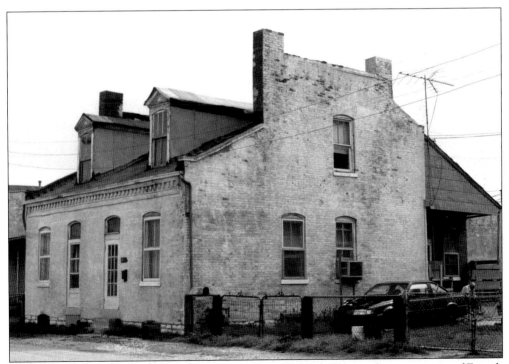
Here is another significant house, found at 4211 2nd Street, whose style seems a mix of French Colonial and Victorian.

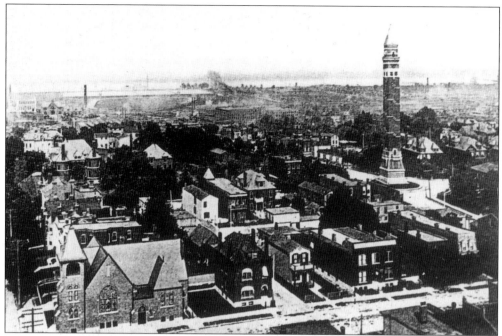

Here is a photo of a Near North neighborhood, *c.* 1912. Notice the Mississippi River in the background.

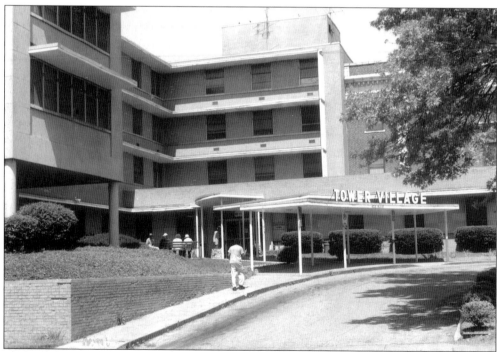

Originally a Jewish Center for the Aged built in 1924 at E. Grand and Blair Avenues, this building is now Tower Village, a nursing home for the elderly. Additions to the front were made in 1959–60.

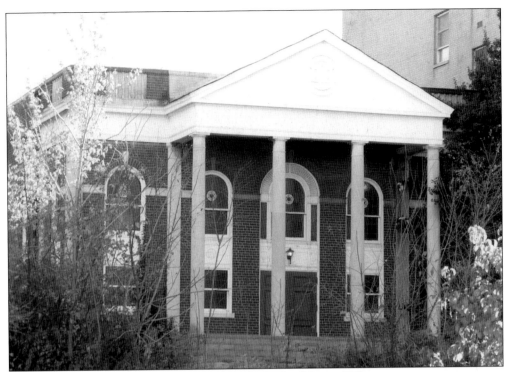

Pictured here is an old synagogue located at the back of Tower Village.

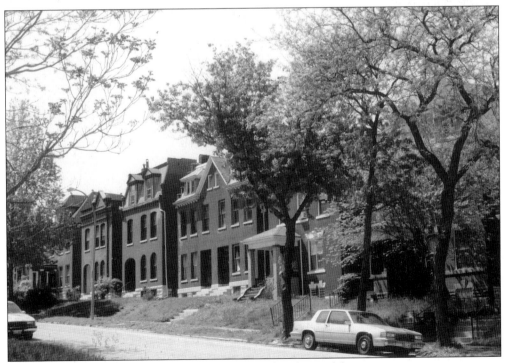

1100 N. Park Place houses a group of residences of quality and finesse.

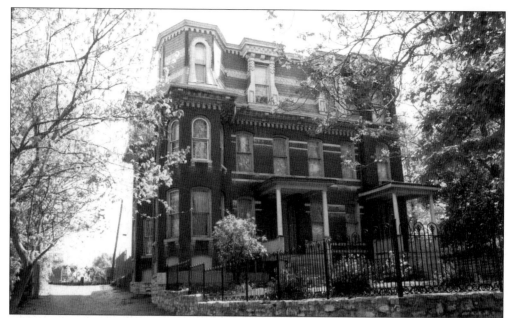

Here is an example of one of the elegant houses in the Park Place area. This large mansion, over-decorated perhaps but nonetheless imposing, was created in the Victorian style of the day, consisting of two-and-a-half stories, dormer windows, and a mansard roof. The iron fence and the stone upon which it stands are also characteristic of the style.

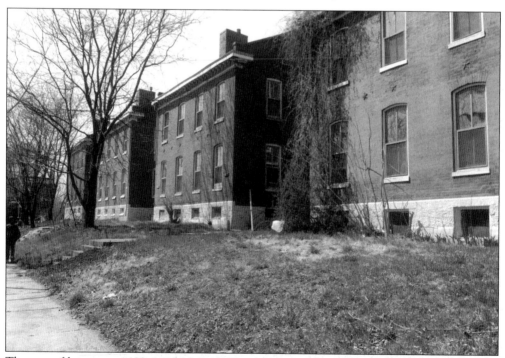

The row of houses at 1400–1410 N. Park Place are not only similar in structure but are free-standing as well. Builder Francis Watkins probably built and ran a hotel in this series of houses, which date back to the late 1800s.

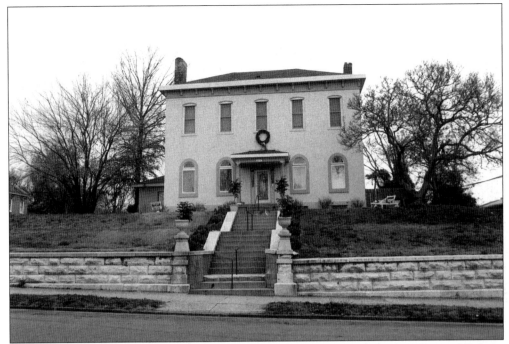

Another house of some stature and beauty is this home at 1129 Penrose Street. With its elaborate portico and tall windows, the house has an air of dignity about it. It was built in 1867.

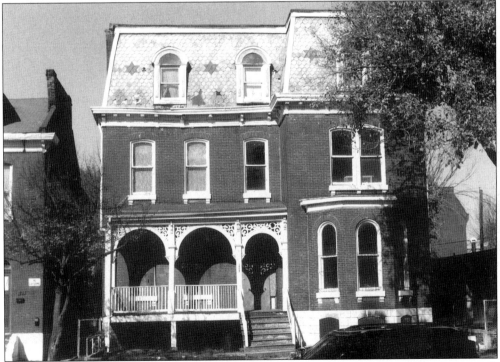

This home at 1907 Bremen Street faces Hyde Park. It is again a Victorian-styled structure with a bay window and upper dormers. It was built in 1879 for Dr. August Rooch.

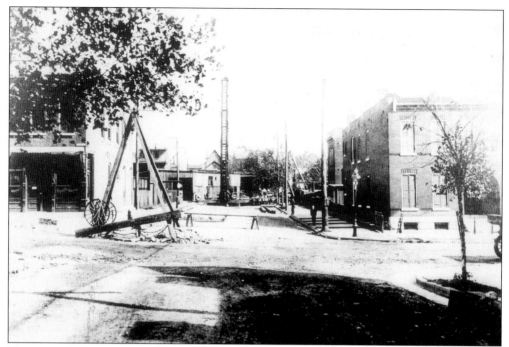

Here is a 1913 image of Ferry Street and Blair Avenue, looking east to Randall Place. (Photo courtesy of Metropolitan Sewer District.)

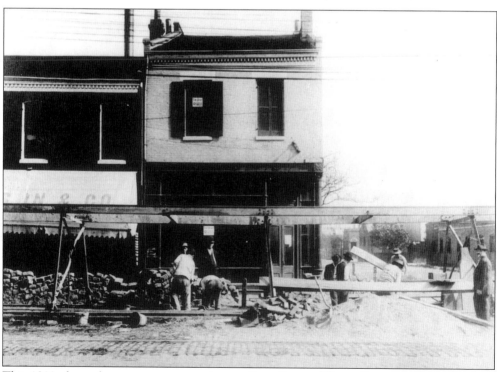

This 1911 photo shows more construction on Ferry Street. (Photo Courtesy of Metropolitan Sewer District.)

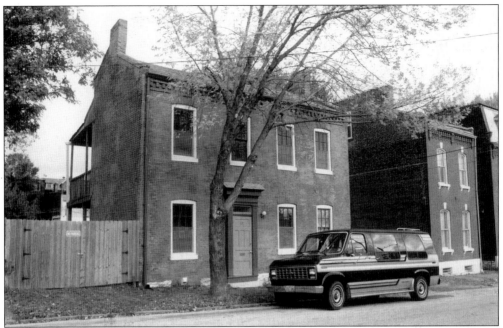

This house at 3616 N. 19th Street was built by a Casper Linck in 1865–66. Its corbelled brick cornice and other details make it an outstanding architectural structure.

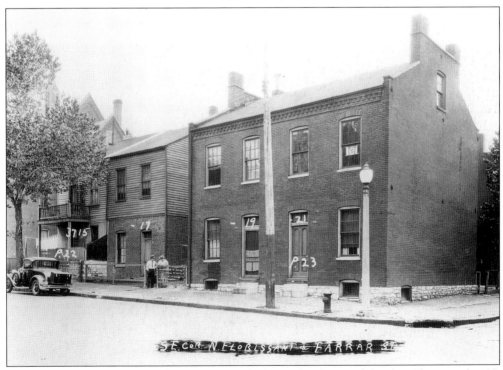

These three buildings demonstrate the nature of the modest home of the day. They stand at N. Florissant Avenue and Farrar Street. (Photo courtesy Special Collections, St. Louis Public Library.)

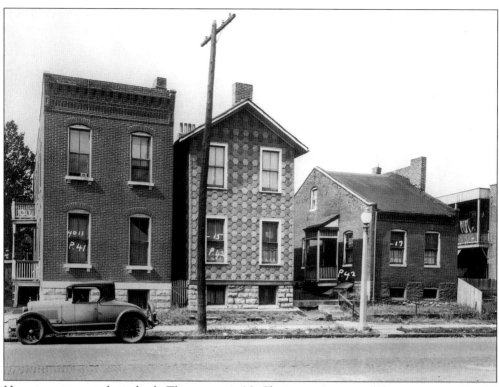

Here is a time-study indeed. The street is N. Florissant Avenue. (Photo courtesy Special Collections, St. Louis Public Library.)

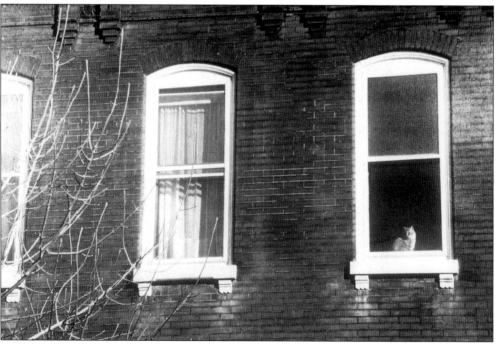

A friend peeps out of the window of an Old North St. Louis home.

Three

GROWING UP IN OLD NORTH ST. LOUIS

One of the loyal stalwarts in Old North St. Louis is Bud Schmidt. Bud's family history goes back to when his grandfather settled in the North St. Louis area. Each succeeding generation has remained in the neighborhood. Bud, and many others like him, have bonded with the neighborhood. In the following pages, we will present an album of pictures that captures what it was like to be born, raised, and to come of age in Old North St. Louis.

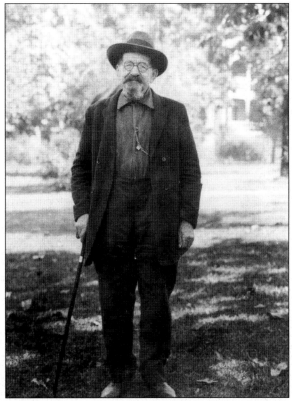

The Schmidt family began with Grandfather Schmidt. This photo dates back to the late 1800s.

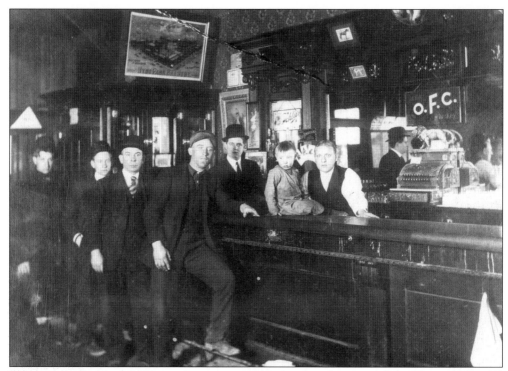

This saloon at 15th and Warren Streets was reputed to be a hangout of the Hogan Gang and Egan's Rats. Seated on the bar with bartender Joseph Schmidt is Bud's brother, Walter. Photo, c. 1910.

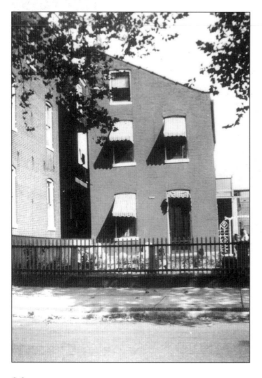

The Schmidt family home at 2708 Blair Avenue was built in the 1850s. Bud was three years old in 1920 when the family moved here from several blocks away.

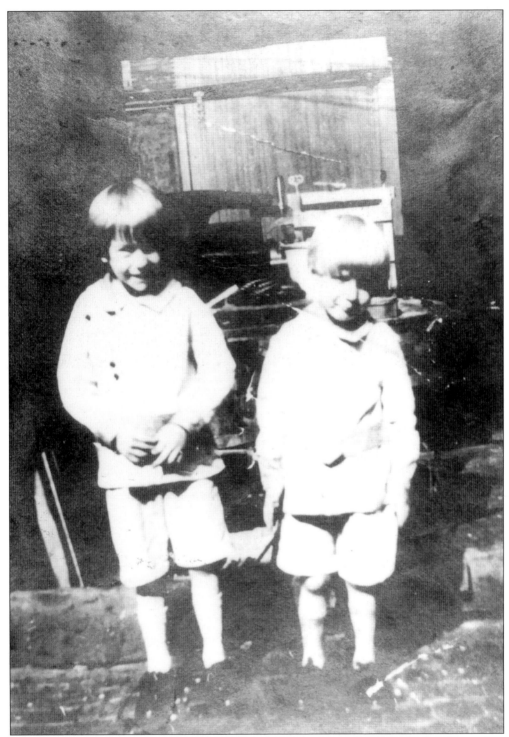

Capturing the ambience of the early 20th century is this photo of Bud and his brother as they stand in front of the family's stable. Bud is shown on the left while his brother Eddie is shown on the right. Photo c. 1926–27.

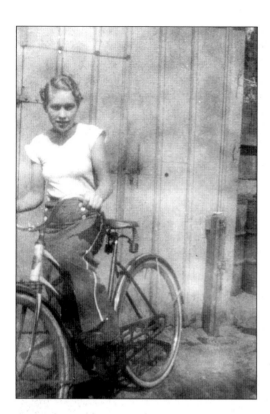

A picture of one of Bud's sisters, Annette, as she appears with her bike . Photo c. 1930.

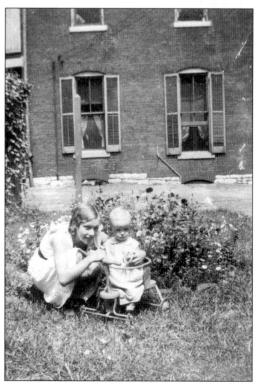

Annette entertains her nephew around 1931 at Blair Avenue and Wright Street.

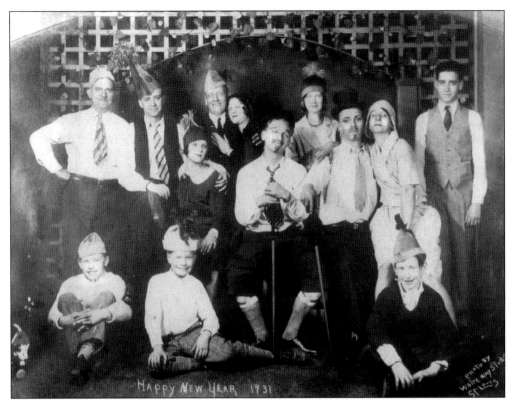

A 1931 New Year's party photo taken at Smith's, a 14th Street photographic studio.

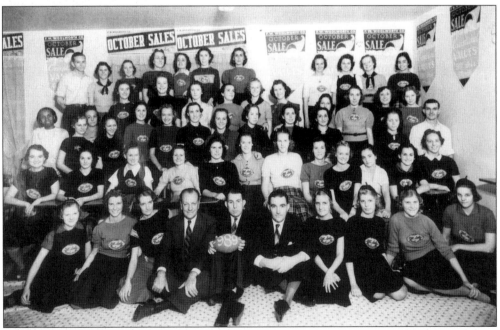

Bud stands in left corner with a group of Woolworth's employees in 1937. This five-and-dime store was located at 14th and Montgomery Streets.

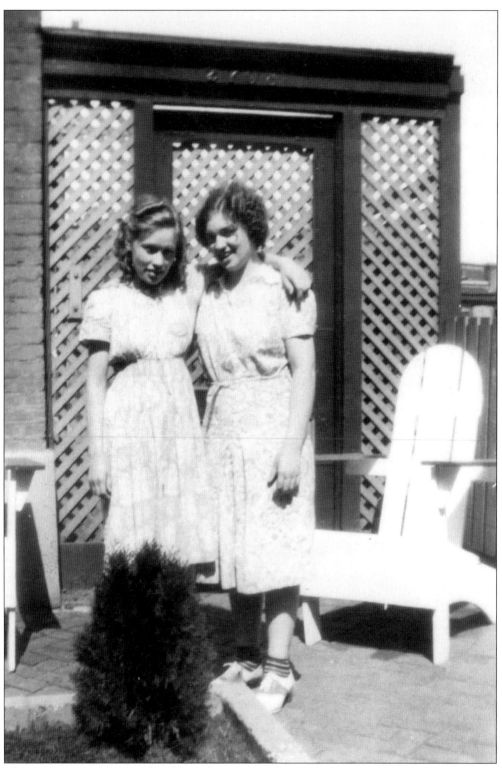

The two sisters Annette and Helen as they appeared *c.* 1938–40.

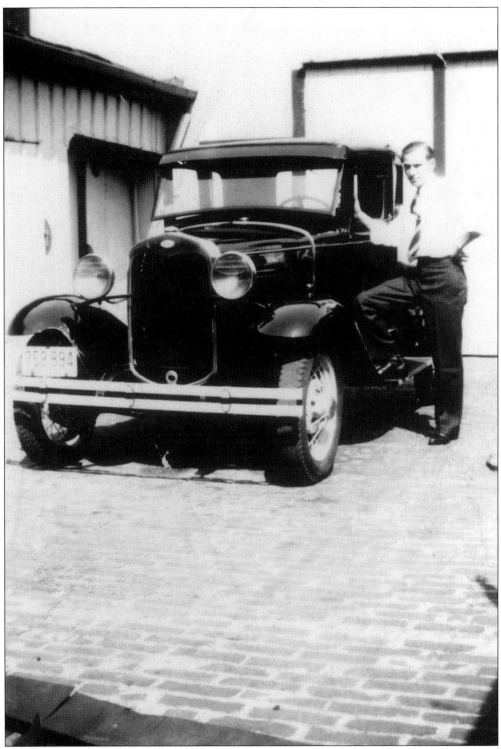

Here is Bud with his prized possession, a Model A Ford. In the background we see glimpses of an outhouse. Photo *c.* 1939–40.

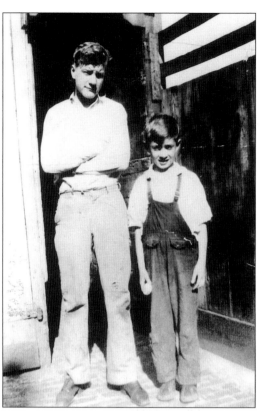

Brother Eddie poses here in the 1930s with a young friend, right, son of a shoe store owner.

Many of the Schmidts and their children gather to celebrate Christmas in the 1940s. Bud stands on the right rear.

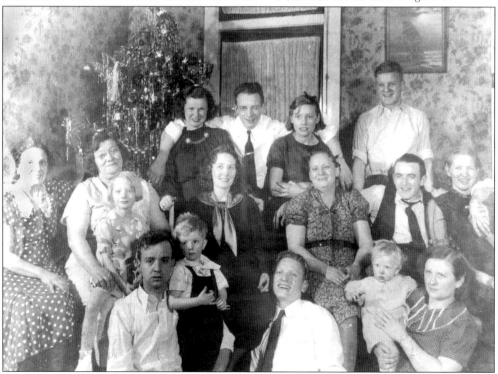

Four

FAMILY LIFE

In order to firmly explore the life and times of the citizens of Old North St. Louis, we turn now to another one of the long-enduring families of the area: the Marx clan. As long-time owners of the Marx Hardware store at 2501 N. 14th Street, they have been leading citizens of the neighborhood. The Marx's roots are long, starting before the Civil War and enduring to the present day.

It is not enough to say that they have experienced life in the neighborhood during its rich and now lean days with steadfastness and loyalty to the area. One must also add that their hardware store has been and continues to be a prevailing landmark in the area. The photos in this chapter revolve around the present-day Marx family and were provided by the current owner of the Marx Hardware, Steve Marx, whose album of North St. Louis provides us with a vivid view of the past.

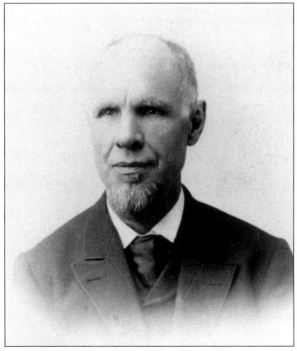

Pictured here is a photo of Frederick W. Marx, the great-great-grandfather of Steve and Andy Marx.

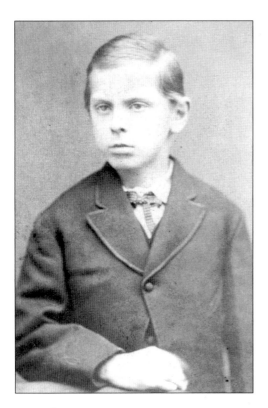

This photo of August Marx, great-grandfather to Steve, was taken in 1878, when August was around ten years old.

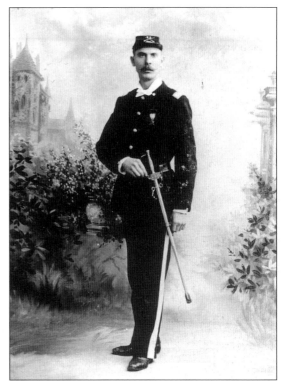

Another photo of August, c. 1895, now a young man and a member of the "Sons of Veterans," which was associated with the Grand Army of the Republic.

In this 1940 photo, August Marx stands in front of the long-time family store at 2501 N. 14th Street.

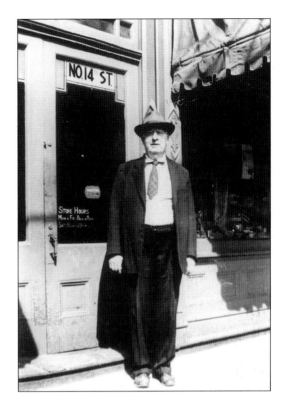

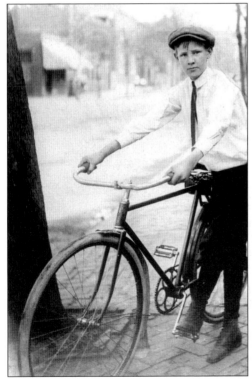

Here is another family member with the same name as a previous Marx, Frederick W. Marx, Steve's grandfather. The picture, c. 1912, was taken at 13th and Warren Streets.

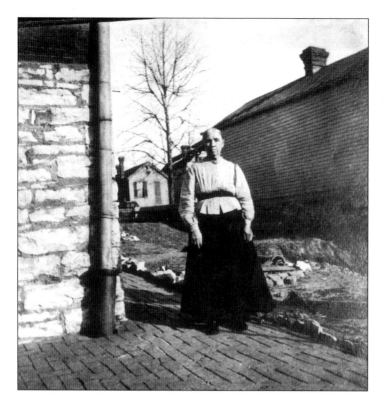

The Neihaus family married into the Marx family. Here is Steve's great-great-grandmother on the Neihaus side. The photo was taken in the late teens.

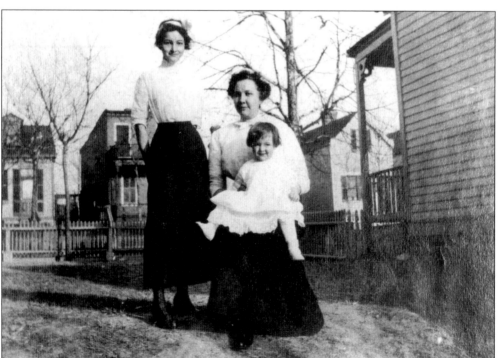

This *c.* 1895 image captures two of the Neihaus women with one of their babies. Minni, to the left, is the great-grandmother to Steve.

Here is Minni in 1928 at 1302 Warren Street. Steve's father is the baby.

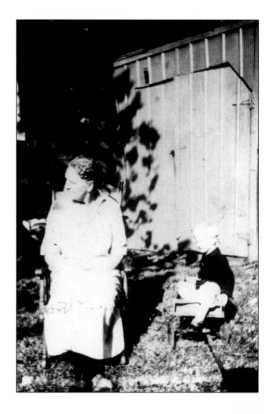

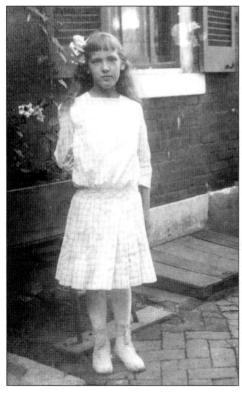

Steve's great aunt, pictured here *c.* 1912–1914, lived at 2517 N. 13th Street.

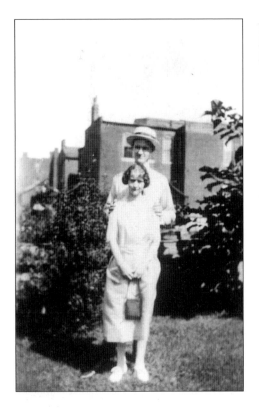

Fred W. Marx and Anna, grandparents of Steve, pose in this photograph at 1302 Warren Street in 1922.

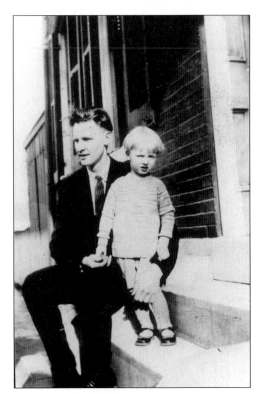

Fred W. Marx, photographed with his child, Steve's father, at 1302 Warren Street, c. 1924–25.

Five
NOTABLE HOUSES

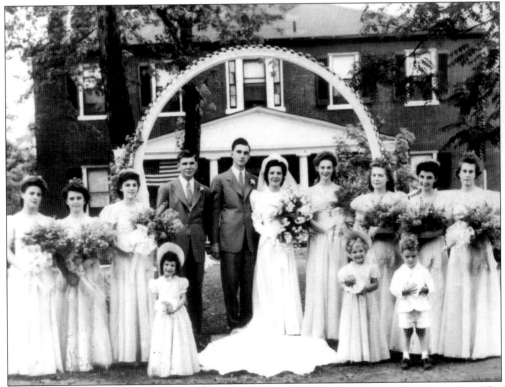

This wedding was held in front of Bissell Mansion during the first half of the 20th century. The historic house, located at 4426 Randall Place, is a gracious adornment in the North St. Louis area. Built in 1823, it is reputed to be the oldest house existing in St. Louis.

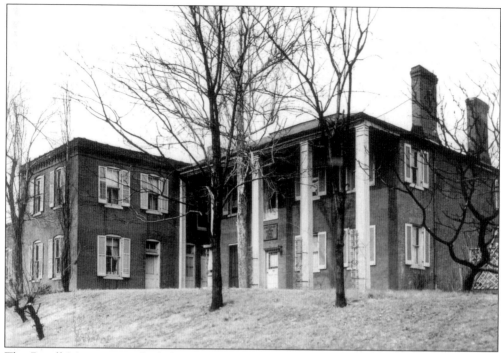

The Bissell Mansion was built by Captain Lewis Bissell and occupied for generations by his relatives. After its rescue from demolition in the 1950s, the mansion was renovated into a restaurant and dinner theater. Pictured here in 1940, the building still displays a majestic air with its white columns and shuttered windows. (Photo courtesy of NPS.)

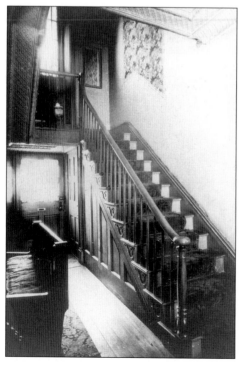

Located on a bluff overlooking the Mississippi, Bissell Mansion displays a style commensurate with the boats that flowed before it. The interior period style is illustrated by a typical staircase with carpeted runs, flowery wall paper, and a platform landing, breaking the stairs' steep climb. (Photo c. 1940, courtesy of NPS.)

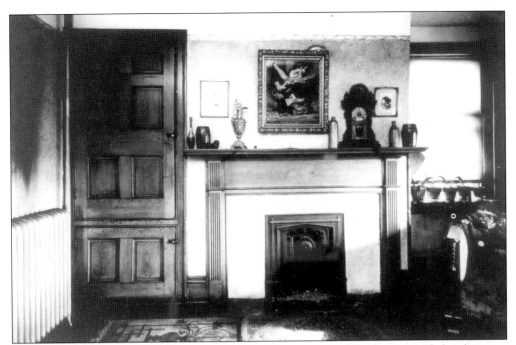

The minimal arrangement of this 1940s Bissell room—a plain mantel and fireplace, an undecorated side door, and uncluttered space—offers a simple, pleasing aesthetic. (Photo courtesy of NPS.)

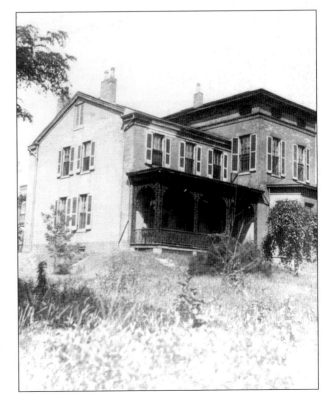

Another important house in the neighborhood was the Beverly Allen home at 1410 E. Grand Avenue. Winston Churchill, the St. Louis writer, made it famous as "Bellegarde" in his novel *The Crisis*. Among those entertained here were notables such as Ulysses S. Grant, W.T. Sherman, and John C. Fremont. Built in 1845, it has since been demolished.

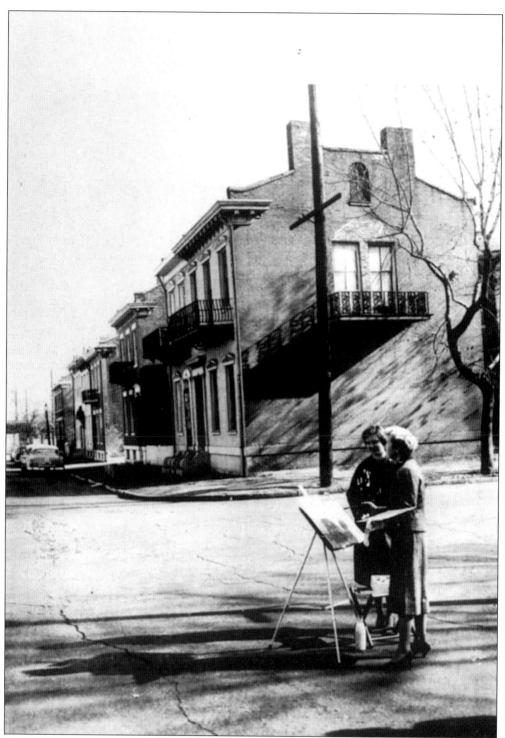

This view shows a typical North St. Louis row of houses on Chambers Street with a series of balconies adorning the front and side of each free-standing home. The painters depicted here seem to have grasped the beauty of these old buildings.

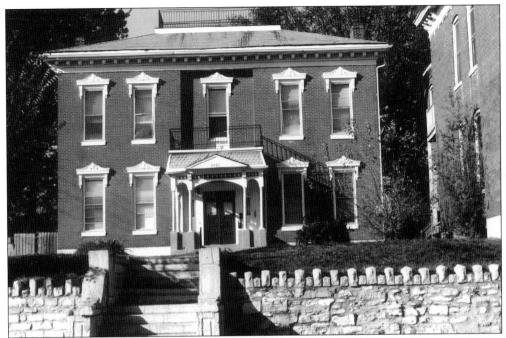

The Shands-Ritchie House at 2223 Salisbury Street easily qualifies as one of the most elegant houses in the area. Built in 1856–57, the home boasts many distinguished features including an ornate entrance and balconies, as well as a balustrade on its roof.

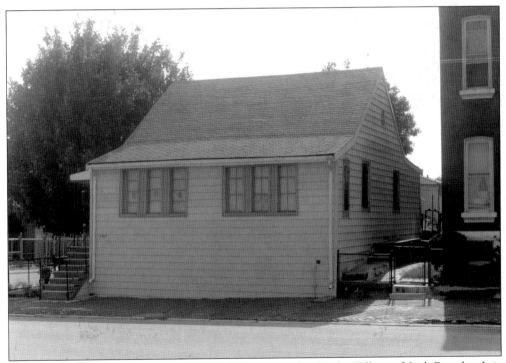

This is an authentic 1820s-style trapper's house, owned today by Tillie and Jack Prouder. It is located in the 3300 block of Klein Street. The original has been considerably modified.

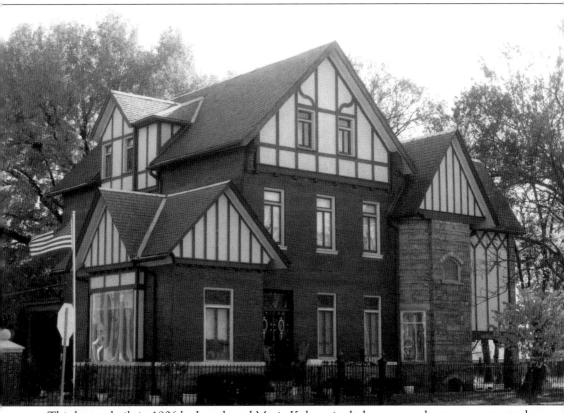

This house, built in 1906 by Joseph and Maria Kulage, includes a tower that was constructed to contain a large organ. Maria's generous endowment in 1928 established the famous "Pink Sisters" convent. It's located at 1904 College Avenue.

Six

CHURCHES

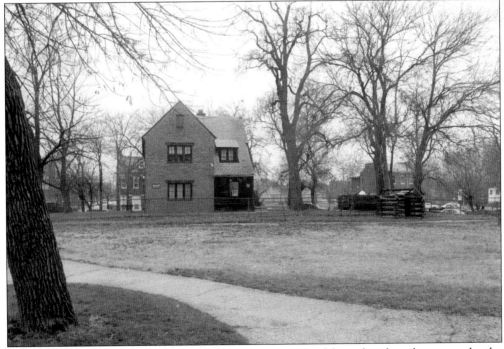

The remains of Marion Place, the public space once reserved for a church and cemetery by the Village of North St. Louis, are located on the present property of Grace Hill House, a neighborhood service organization.

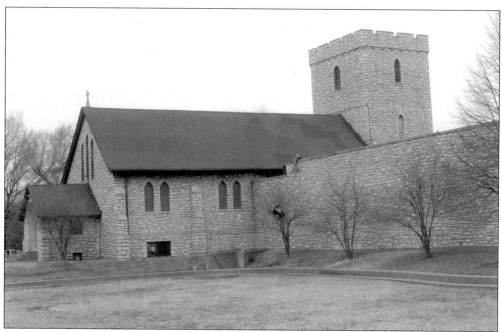

Still sitting on Marion Place of the old Village of North St. Louis, Grace Episcopal Church has seen many changes to its exterior. However, its social service to the poor has not diminished since it assumed the status of a mission in 1910. The church itself is no longer active.

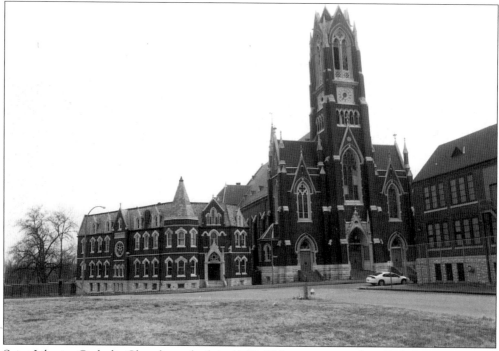

Saint Liborius Catholic Church was built in 1888–89 by immigrants from Paderborn, Germany. Its pointed windows, towers, and long spire define the German Gothic style. Located at 1835 N. 18th Street, it is no longer active as a Catholic church.

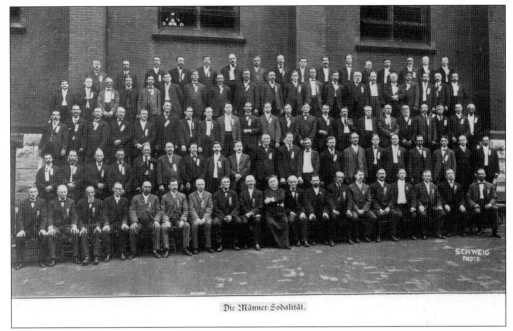

Die Männer-Sodalität.

Here is a group photograph of the many members of the Men's Sodality of St. Liborius, *c.* 1906.

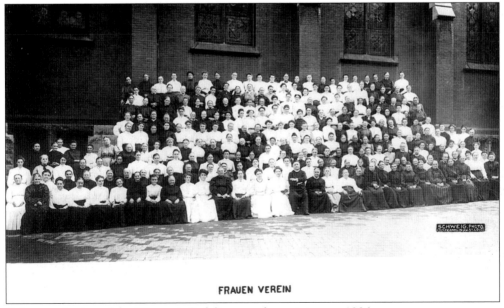

FRAUEN VEREIN

A large gathering of the Women's Sodality pose for a picture, *c.* 1906.

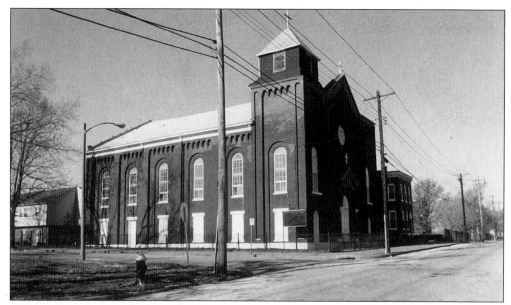

STS. Cyril and Methodius Polish National Catholic Church at 2005 N.11th Street is the most historically interesting of all the churches in the neighborhood. It was established by disaffected Catholic separatists who left the other Polish Catholic churches in St. Louis. This rebellious group was liberal and allowed priests to marry. The building, erected in 1857, was previously occupied by the North Presbyterian Church.

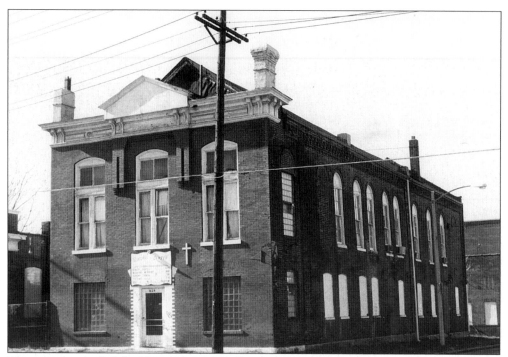

This structure, called the New Center, has elements both of the classical and the Romanesque in its architectural design. Located at 14th and Howard Streets, it was built by the First German Society for those who followed the teachings of Emmanuel Swedenborg.

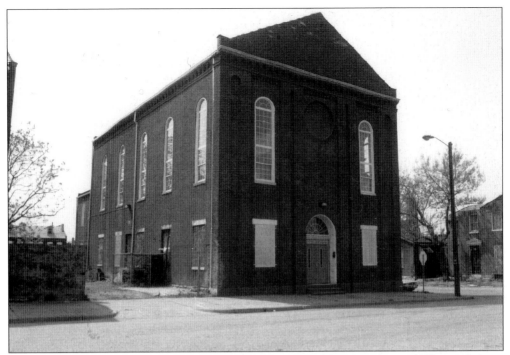

Pictured here, the True Life United Pentecostal church building, at Blair and Warren Streets, once played an important role in North St. Louis as the Zion German Evangelical Lutheran Church. It was built in 1860.

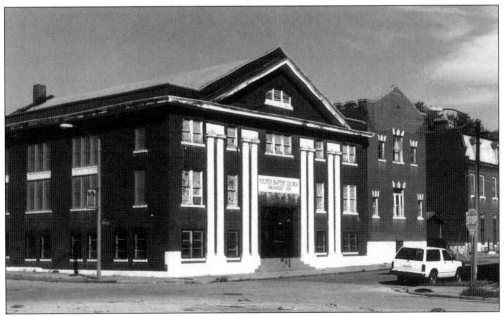

Fourth Baptist Church at 2901 13th Street was erected in 1923. It was organized, however, as early as 1851. The church has been active in the community for many years.

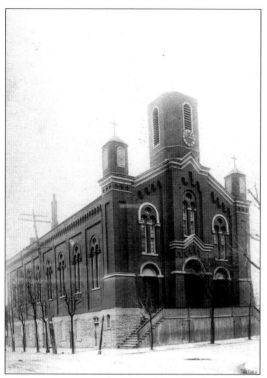

To many, Holy Trinity Catholic Church at 14th and Mallinckrodt Streets is the finest church in North St. Louis. It was erected by the Germans in 1848 as a German-language parish. Over the years, it was rebuilt on two separate occasions. The church shown here is the second of these structures. It was constructed in 1857.

The Holy Trinity Church, with its glittering twin 120-foot towers, has become a landmark. Of French Gothic design, it is built largely of limestone. Interior patterns make it an architectural gem. It was built in 1898 on the same site as the second erected church.

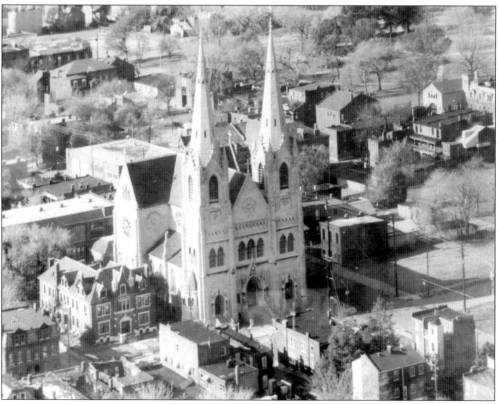

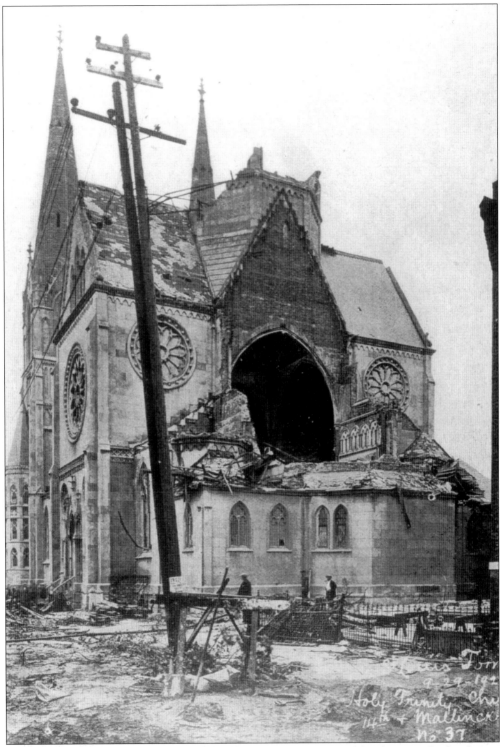

Here again is the Holy Trinity Church, though this time damaged by the tornado that hit on September 29, 1927.

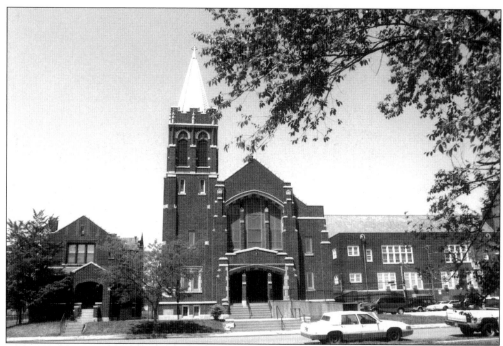

Another German establishment is St. Paul's Lutheran Church at 1904 E. College Avenue. The first church was built in 1862, a short distance from the site of the present church.

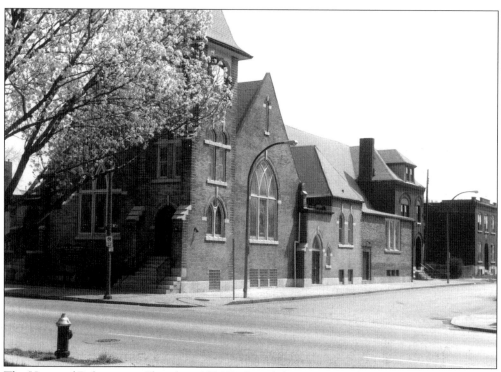

The House of Deliverance Church at 1524 E. Grand Avenue is amply supplied with roofs; here are three of them, all individually designed.

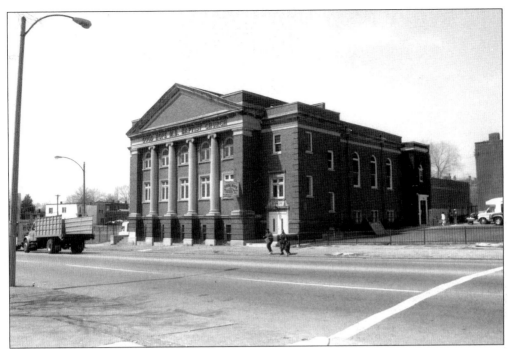

This massive structure, currently the Good Hope Missionary Baptist Church, stands with its classically designed columns at 2115 E. Grand Avenue.

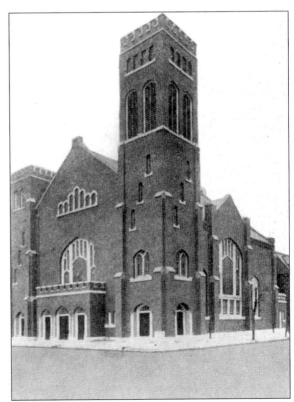

The Frieden German Evangelical Church, which stands at 1908 Newhouse Avenue, was one of the popular churches in the area. The parish served the spiritual needs of young and old people. This second building was erected in 1907–1908.

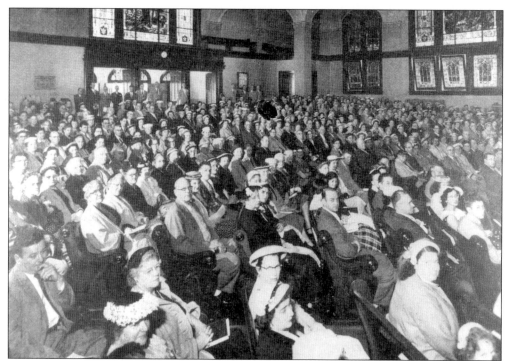

To demonstrate the popularity of the Frieden church, one could point to photos such as this one that captures the enormity of the audience at a service.

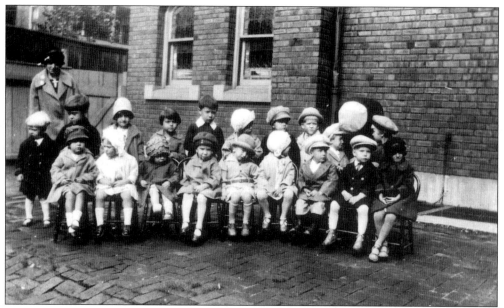

The Sunday School building across the street from the church itself was later turned into Friedens Haus, a community-service organization that contributed to the needs of the poor. Here we catch a glimpse of a Sunday school class in 1925–26, attended by toddlers.

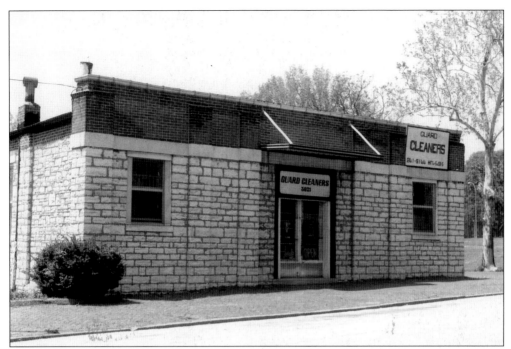

Pictured here is the stone understructure of Bethlehem Evangelical Lutheran Church, built in 1858 at 19th and Salisbury Streets. The second floor was destroyed by the 1927 tornado.

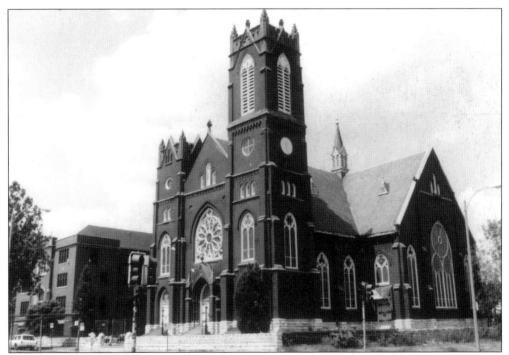

The Third Bethlehem Church at 2153 Salisbury was badly damaged by fire soon after it was built in 1893. It was rebuilt in 1895. In 1927, it suffered tornado damage when one of its towers was blown away.

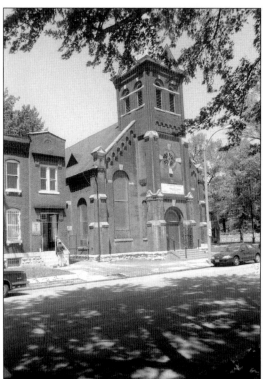

This building has been home to St. John's United Church of Christ since 1887. It is now St. James Community Center located at 1507 E. College Avenue.

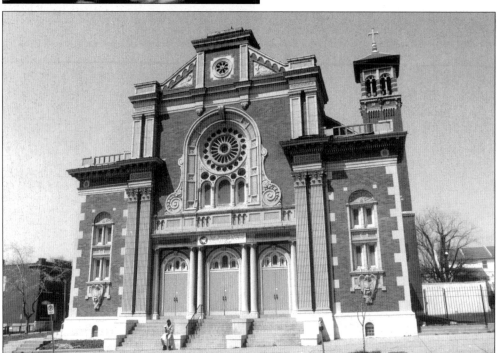

This Gothic structure with its rose window and large tower was originally the Holy Name Catholic Church. It later became the New Jerusalem Cathedral Church of God in Christ. This architectural prize is one of the finest churches in the neighborhood. It is located at 2047 E. Grand Avenue.

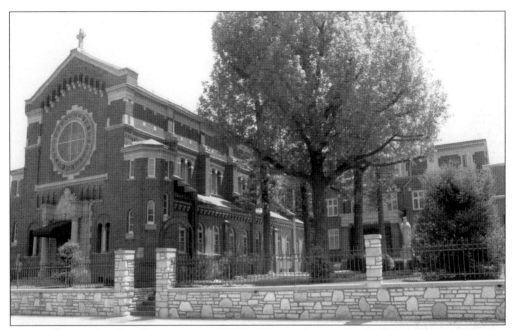

Mount Grace Chapel and Convent at 1438 E. Warne Avenue is another architectural beauty of Near North St. Louis. Home to the celebrated "Pink Sisters" nuns who devote their lives to silence and prayer, it has been a sacred retreat for many St. Louisans.

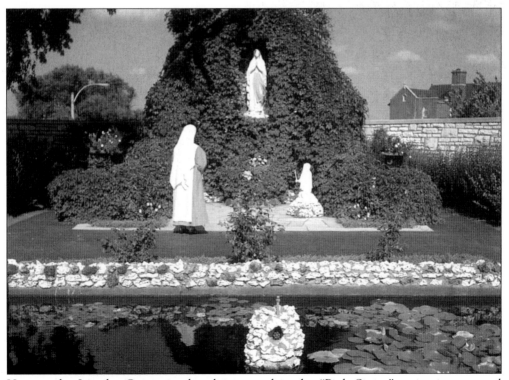

Here at the Lourdes Grotto in the cloister garden, the "Pink Sisters" maintain perpetual adoration of the Blessed Sacrament.

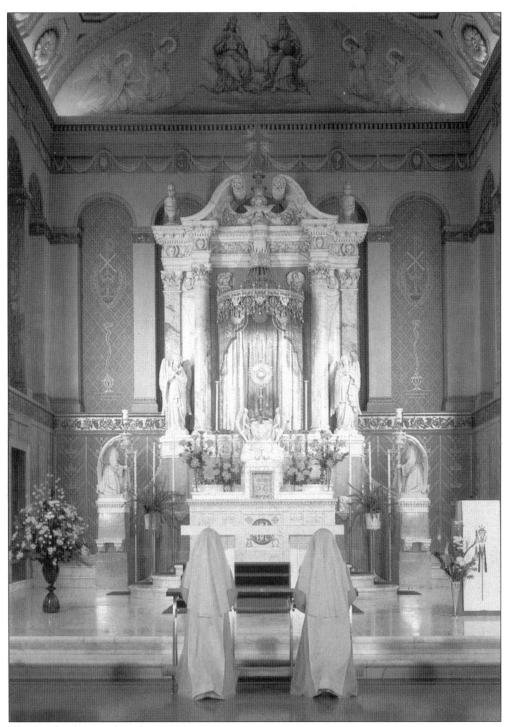

The lovely cloister chapel is open to visitors.

Seven

SCHOOLS

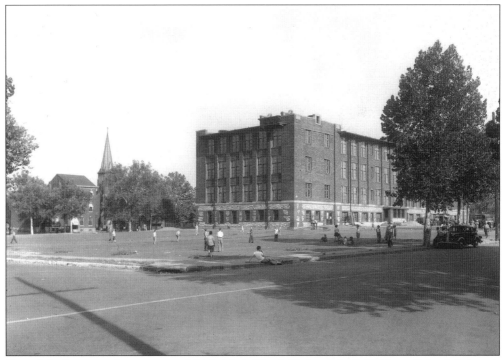

One of the largest and most successful schools in North St. Louis is the Webster School. It is now located on the grounds of the third circle, laid out as Clinton Place for a school for the Village of North St. Louis. That circle no longer exists, but Webster has thrived handsomely on its site. The building shown is not the first of the Webster schools. It was constructed in 1906.

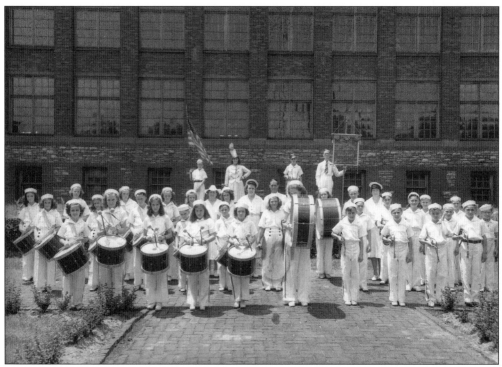

Pictured here is the 1940 Webster School's Drum and Bugle Corps at parade rest.

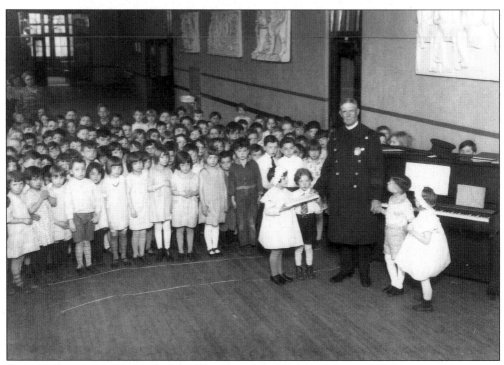

Young folks say goodbye to their traffic officer, Mr. King, in February 1930.

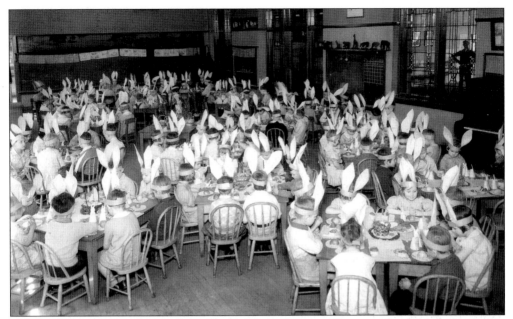

There are plenty of bunnies gathered here to help celebrate Easter at the Webster School in April 1934. Despite the bleak economic times of the 1930s, this group seems to be well-dressed and nourished.

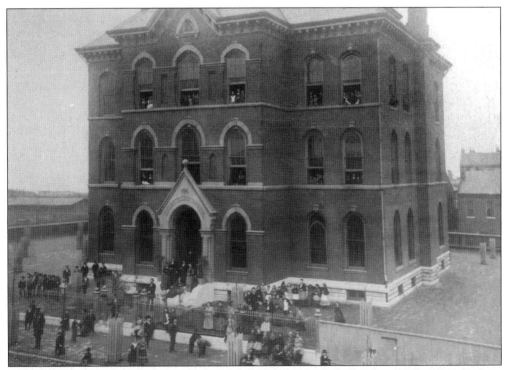

This 1876 photograph depicts the Ames School, built in North St. Louis in 1873. After the furor of the Civil War had died down, St. Louis constructed several new schools, including this one. (Special Collections, St. Louis Public Library.)

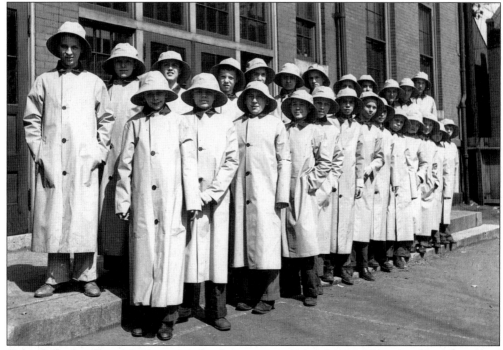

Ames School traffic patrol boys pose for their portrait in April 1940. The school had flourished mightily from its beginning years.

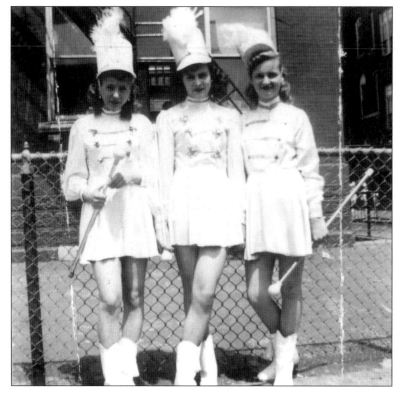

Ames School in 1953 proudly presents three highly costumed majorettes, one of whom is Mary Ann Tyra, whom we have met previously in the vicinity.

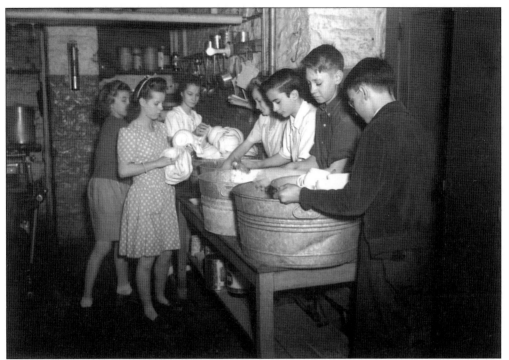

In November 1944, a group of Ames School students line up to wash dishes.

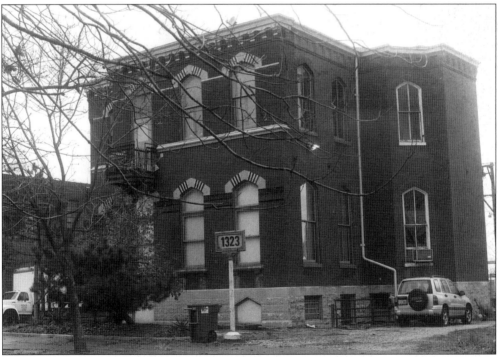

Since St. Louisan Miss Susan Blow popularized the kindergarten, most grade schools have had a kindergarten appended to it. Here is one that had been attached to the old Ames School.

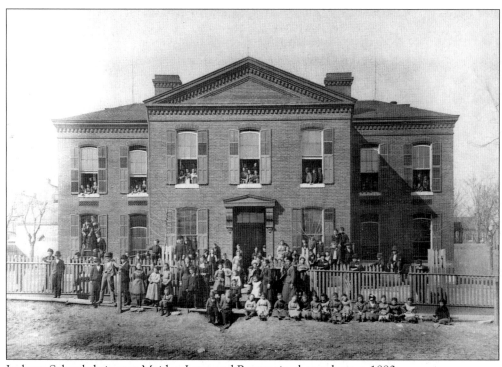

Jackson School thrives at Maiden Lane and Reservoir, shown here *c.* 1880.

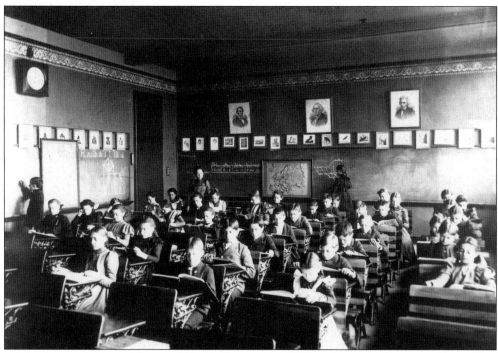

One is struck by the number of students that seem to fill every seat in this large classroom at Jackson School's new location at 1632 Hogan Street. Photo *c.* 1904.

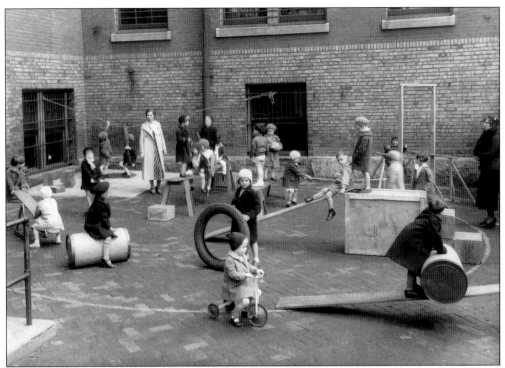

Children play at recess in a Jackson School playground in May 1934.

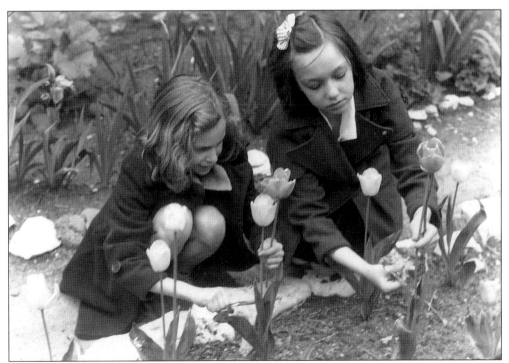

Here are two bonnie lasses in a tulip bed at Jackson School in May 1939. It may well be that this was instruction in a gardening class.

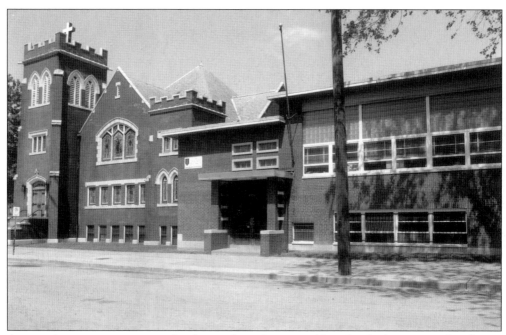

Among the many innovations that have taken place in public school education is the charter school. The African American Rite of Passage School conducts classes at 4032 22nd Street. Formerly, Markus Lutheran Church (1912) and school occupied these buildings.

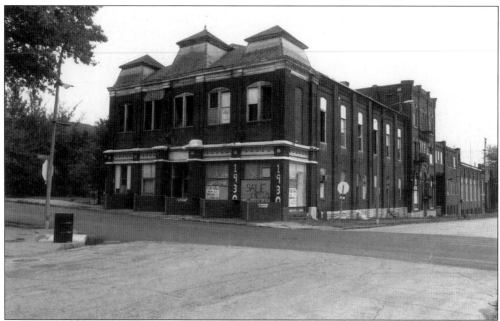

One of the features that has gained much praise is this North St. Louis Turnverein, home of the North St. Louis Turners. This German athletic club, at 1928 Salisbury Street, has long proven to be the center of German social life in the area with its emphasis on gymnastic and other social activities. The first building on this site was completed in 1879. The complex currently awaits renovation.

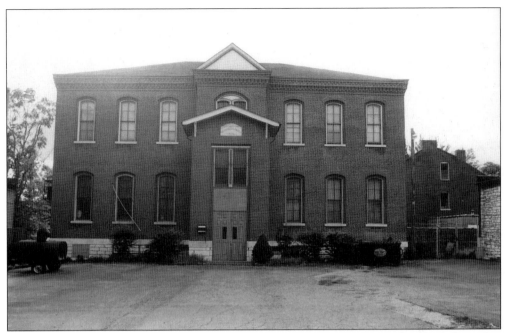

Pictured here is the German School for Bethlehem Evangelical Lutheran Church, dedicated in 1872. Located at 3615 N. 19th Street, it provided its parishioners with instruction in the German language. Like some churches in the area, there was a school attached to it.

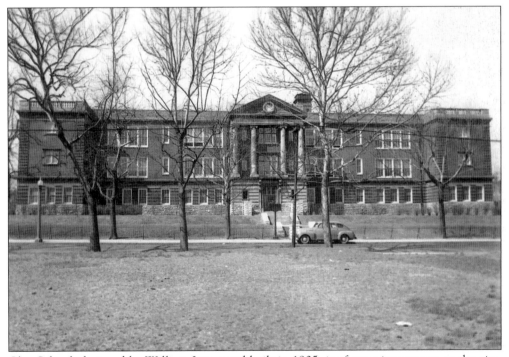

Clay School, designed by William Ittner and built in 1905, is of great importance to the city. Located at 3820 N. 14th Street, it was created in the grand, Greek revival style. It appears here in April 1952.

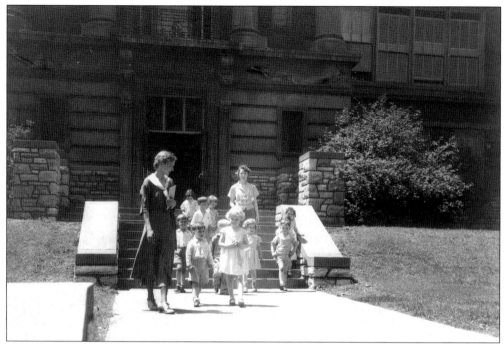

Toddlers attend the Clay school in May 1934.

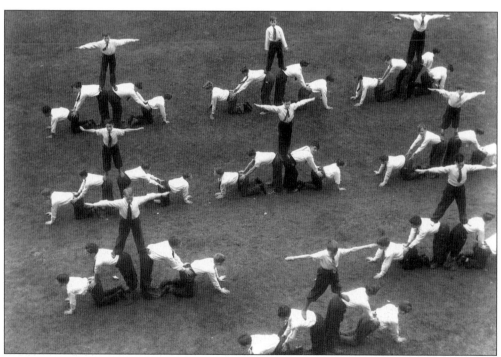

Students at the Clay School in April 1939 perform gymnastic feats by creating human pyramids.

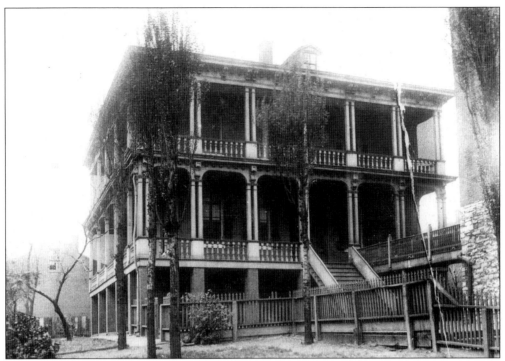

This building opened in the spring of 1849 as the rectory of the Holy Trinity Catholic Church. On the first floor, 13 students were enrolled in the first church school of the parish.

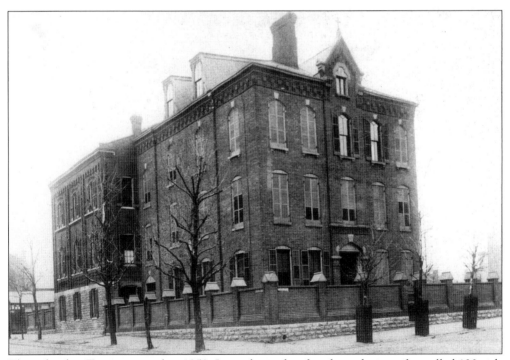

This school at Trinity opened in 1859. It was limited to female students and enrolled 120 girls in 1860. It was built at Mallinckrodt Street and Blair Avenue.

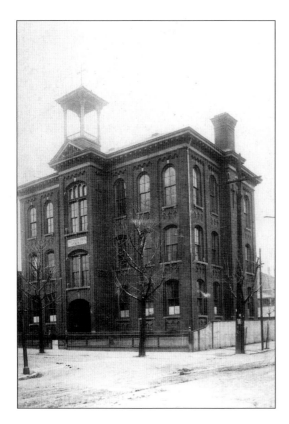

This Holy Trinity Catholic School, pictured here in 1871 at 14th and Mallinckrodt Streets, was a school opened exclusively for boys. The grounds are now used as a playground.

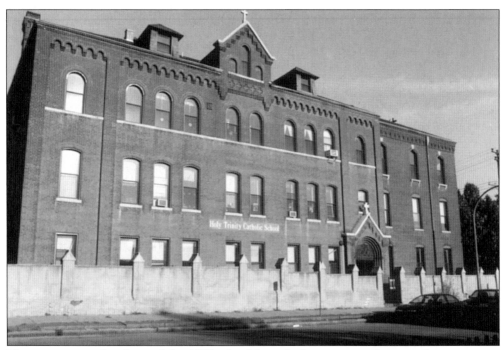

Here is a present-day photo of the 1859 school for girls. It is now co-educational.

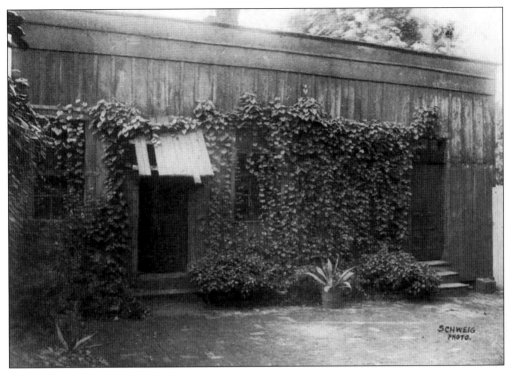

This first school was an early center of the St. Liborius parish.

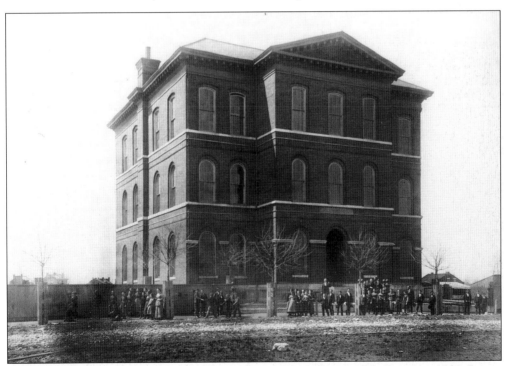

This is an early photo of the Irving School located at 3829 N. 25th Street, *c.* 1880. It was erected in 1871.

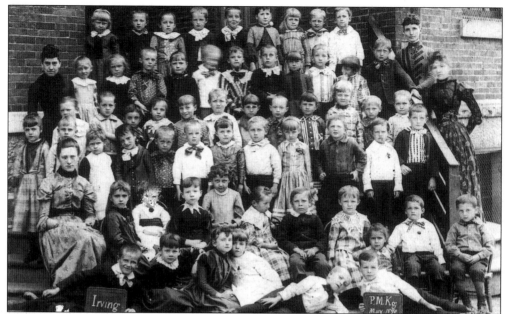

Here is a period study for you! While looking at this Irving School kindergarten class in 1890, do you heed the quaint clothing of the youngsters and the dress of their teachers?

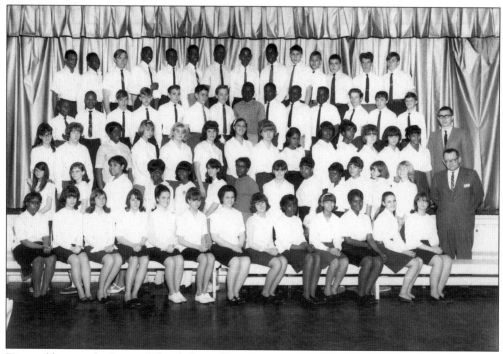

Pictured here is the Irving School class of June 1968.

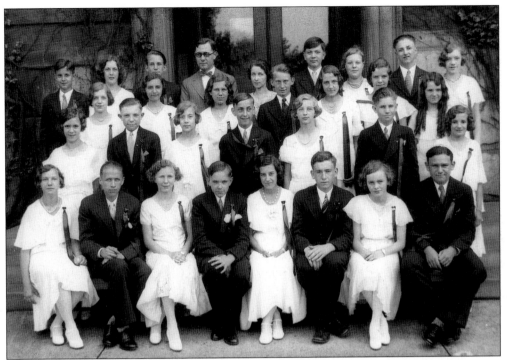

The 1931 graduating class of Eliot School is due a load of congratulations!

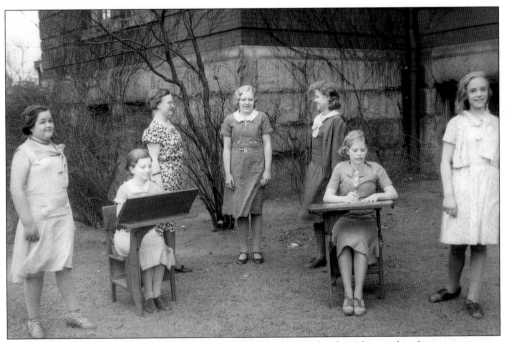

In a class at Eliot School in March 1933, students are involved in the study of proper posture. From what we have witnessed so far—gardening instruction, posture care, gymnastics—the schools of yesteryear seem to have had an excellent curriculum that was advantageous to the growth of the whole child.

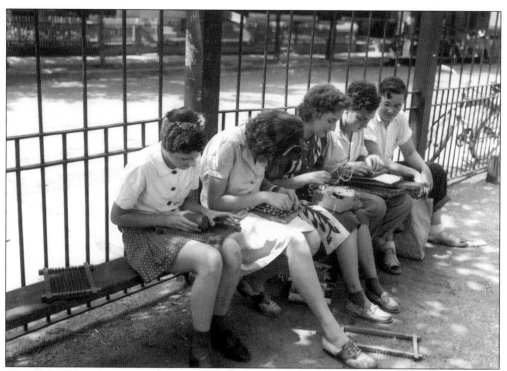

Pictured here is a summer scene at Eliot School playground in July 1942.

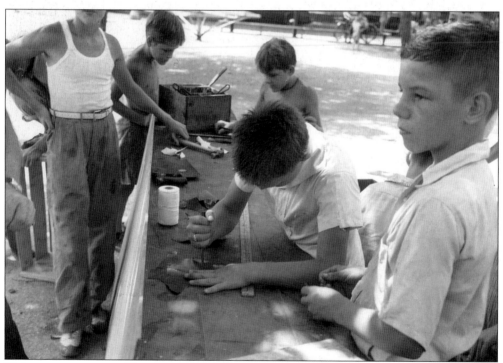

This summer scene at Eliot School in July 1942 illustrates that there is more here for these youngsters than fun and games.

Eight

PARKS

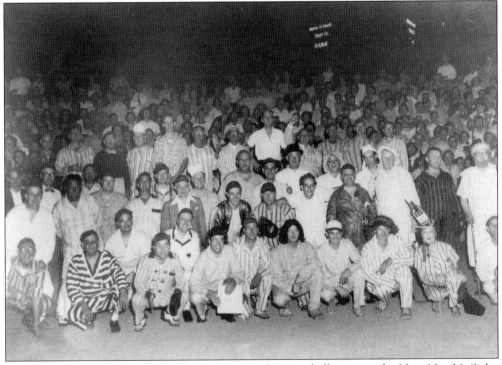

A crowd of St. Louis Business Men's Association fans at a ball game at the Near North's Sisler Park. It was named after George Sisler, who was considered the greatest player in the history of the old St. Louis Browns. The park was located at E. Grand and N. Florissant Avenues. The time was September, 1948.

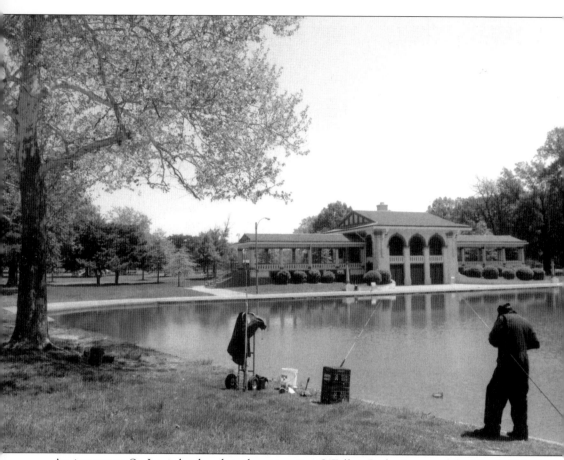

An important St. Louis landmark is the attractive O'Fallon Park. A gem of the North Side, it was built on the grounds of philanthropist John O' Fallon, a 19th-century businessman who left millions to various city institutions.

Here is a glimpse of a family enjoying the greenery of O'Fallon Park early in the 20th century.

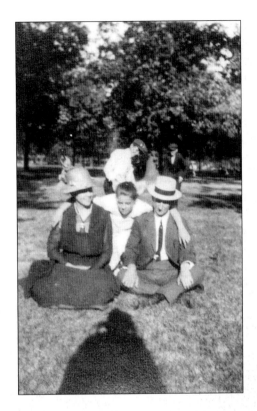

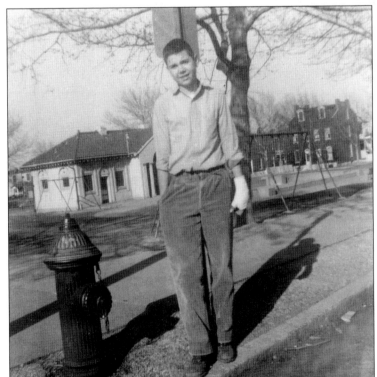

Another significant site in North St. Louis is Strodtman Park. Pictured here is a young man from the 1950s, Fred Hale, posing on the park grounds that face Palm Street between 13th and 14th Streets.

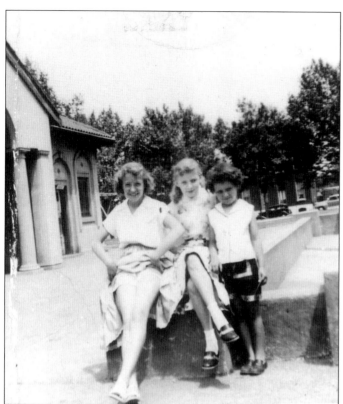

Here in this vintage shot of Strotman Park in 1952, Mary Ann Tyra is encircled by "Laverne & Shirley."

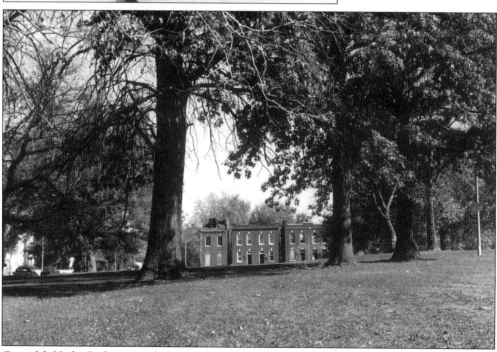

Graceful Hyde Park, one of the region's most historical sites, is chock full of historical memories. Here we view a recent photograph.

Nine
ST. LOUIS PLACE

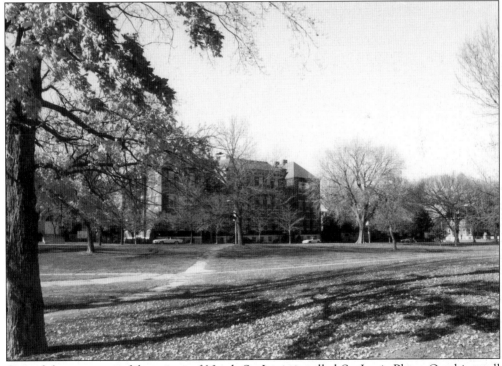

One of the more graceful sections of North St. Louis is called St. Louis Place. On this small space are gathered some of the finest Victorian homes in the neighborhood. These fine homes continue onto side streets and St. Louis Avenue. These apartments on St. Louis Place have been created out of the old Blair School building, erected in the 1880s and 1890s.

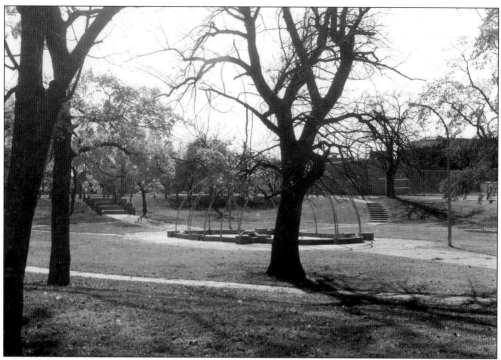

This symmetrically arranged park adorns St. Louis Place.

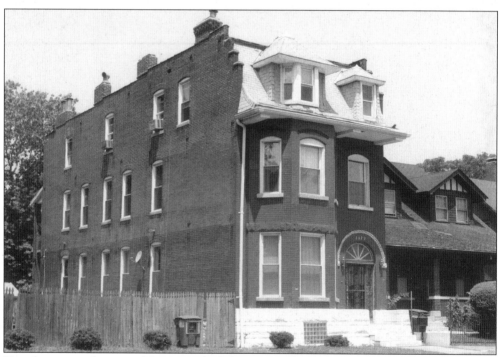

Two dormer windows, an elaborate arched doorway, and tall windows provide this home on St. Louis Place with a slight Victorian flavor.

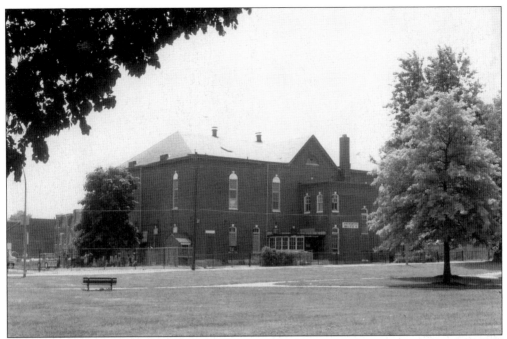

The Youth and Family Center at 2930 St. Louis Place was formerly a German school built in the late 1800s.

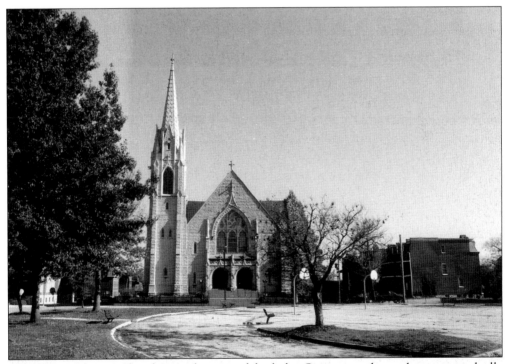

The Zion Lutheran Church was the second built by German settlers, who were gradually acquiring wealth. The first church, built in 1860, was a meager affair that cost very little. The second structure, built in 1895 by German architect Albert Knell, cost quite a bit more.

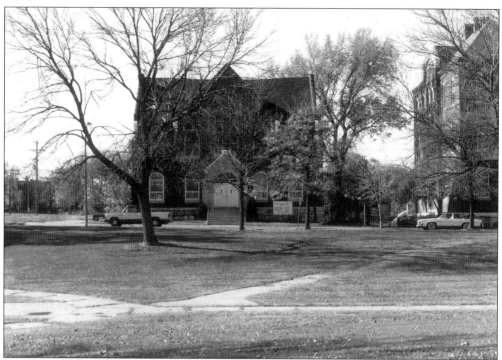

With a simple-face and Gothic echoes, the St. Louis Park Baptist Church is located at 2629 St. Louis Place.

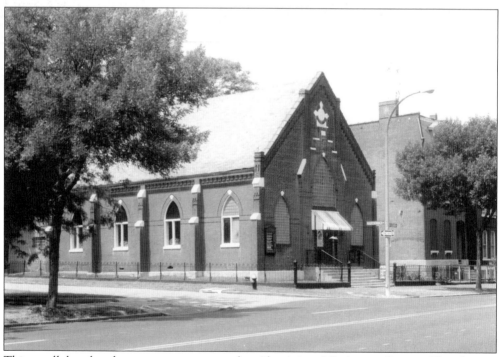

This small but handsome structure, now the Abyssinian Missionary Baptist Church, was established as the Second German Swedenborgian Church in 1883.

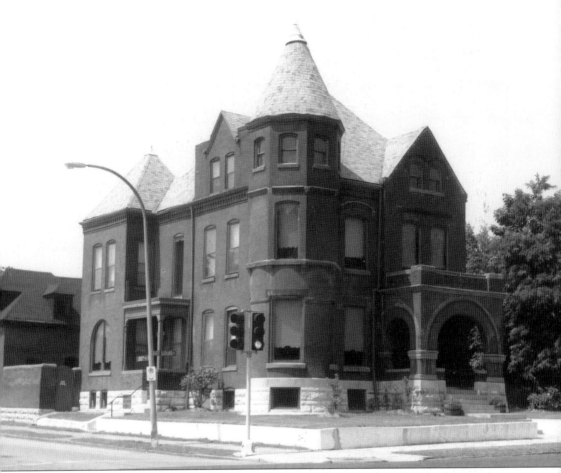

Around the corner from St. Louis Place stands this residence with a Queen Anne tower, pitched roofs, and elaborate entrance way. It is easily one of the most prominent homes in the area.

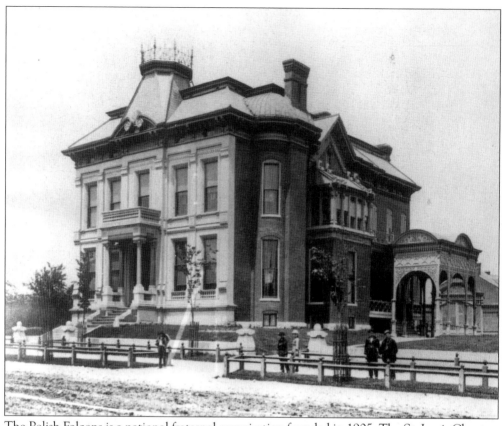

The Polish Falcons is a national fraternal organization founded in 1905. The St. Louis Chapter, Nest 45, has been based in the old Stifel mansion since 1932.

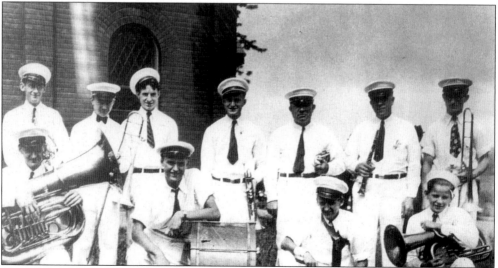

The Falcons' Nest 45 marching band marches proudly in 1932.

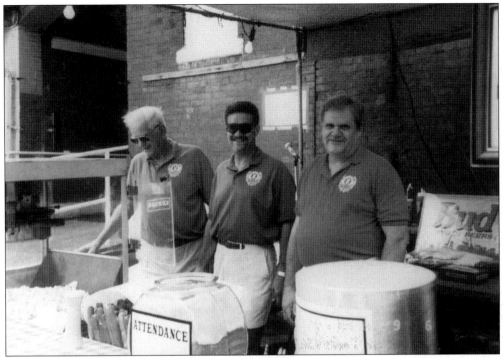

Pictured here is a view of the Polish festivities held by the Falcons in 1996.

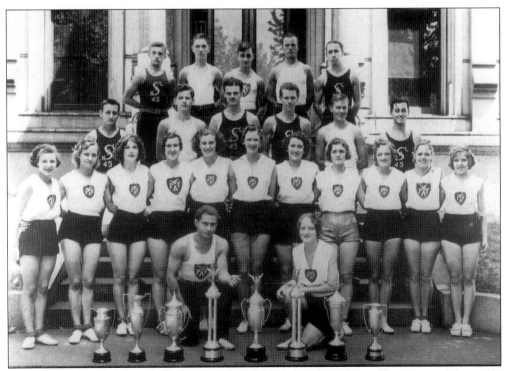

Among the activities encouraged and sponsored by the Falcons are sporting groups. The group seen here is posing in the 1930s with their trophies.

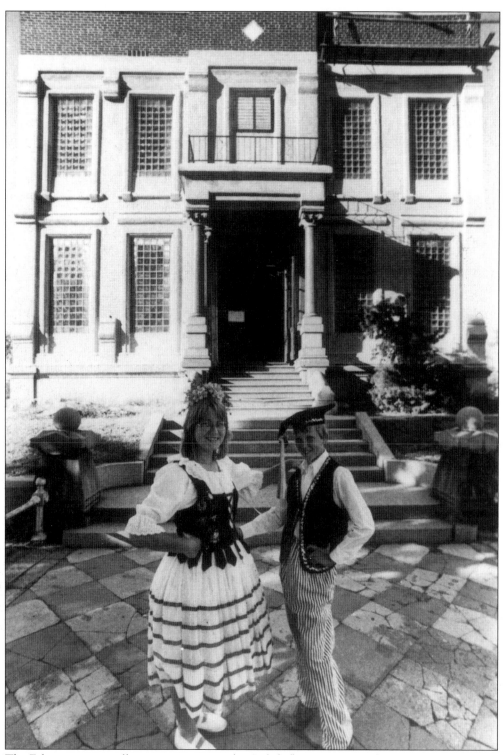

The Falcons occasionally sponsor events with a Polish flavor. Here are dancers posing in native costume for a festival held in the 1980s.

Ten

COMMERCE
AND INDUSTRY

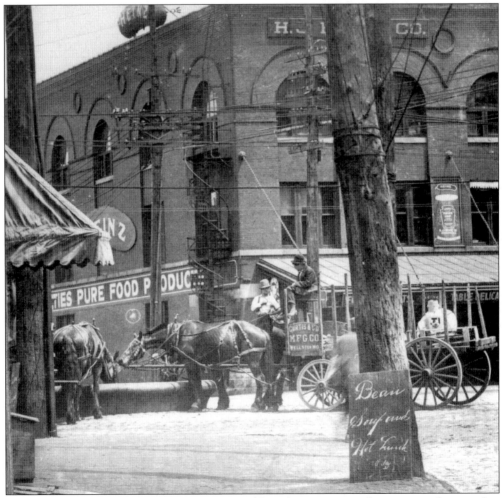

Horses and wagons along busy Cass Avenue and Broadway transport the many goods created in the Near North neighborhood.

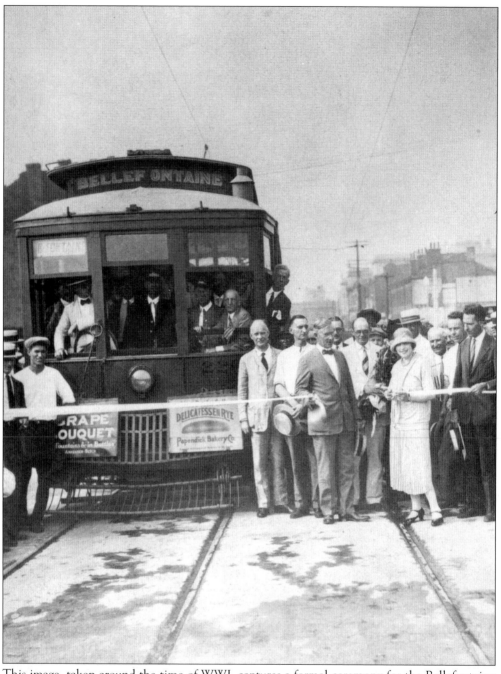

This image, taken around the time of WWI, captures a formal ceremony for the Bellefontaine streetcar line.

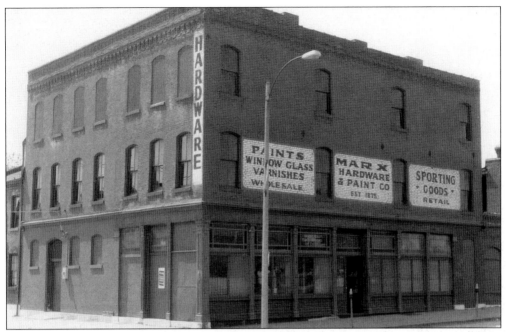

This company at 2501 N. 14th Street has developed into a North St. Louis icon: the Marx Hardware store. It has endured unchanged for generations and is a symbol of longevity and loyalty for the entire neighborhood. This block of 14th Street was part of the famed 14th Street Shopping District. The Bellefontaine streetcar ran down 14th Street .

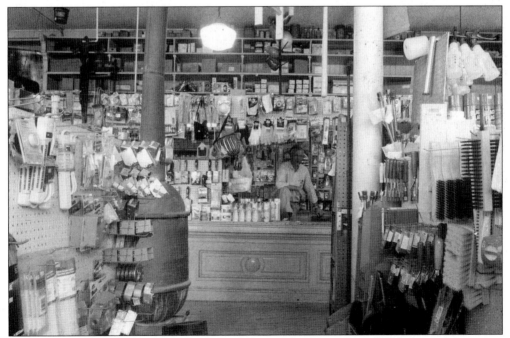

The Marx Hardware store has existed in this same fashion more-or-less since its founding, warmed by the pot-bellied stove and brimming with merchandise. Steve Marx himself waits for more customers.

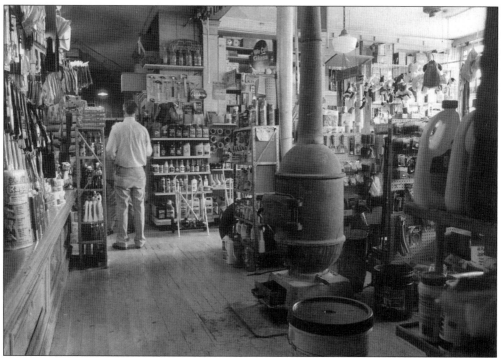

The shelves are crowded in this view of the store's well-stocked interior.

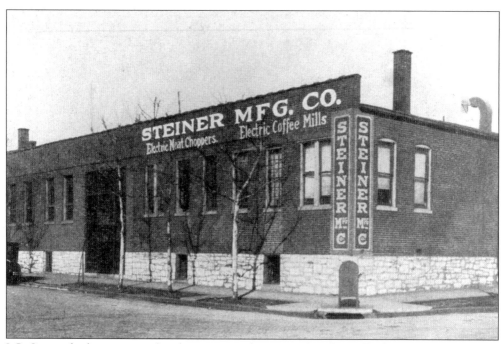

J.C. Steiner had patents on the electric meat chopper and coffee mill which he maintained at this plant, located on N. 14th Street, near the 14th Street shopping district.

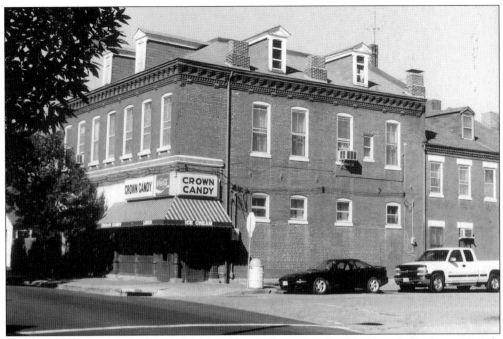

Every day, crowds flock to one of the most revered sites in all of St. Louis: the Crown Candy Kitchen at 14th Street and St. Louis Avenue. This eatery has become a St. Louis-must since it opened in 1913.

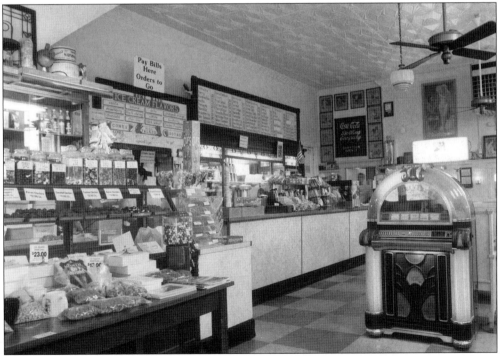

An interior shot of the candy company with its simple setting and old-fashioned items shows an antique fan rivaling a jukebox for attention. The candy cases are eye-catchers, as well.

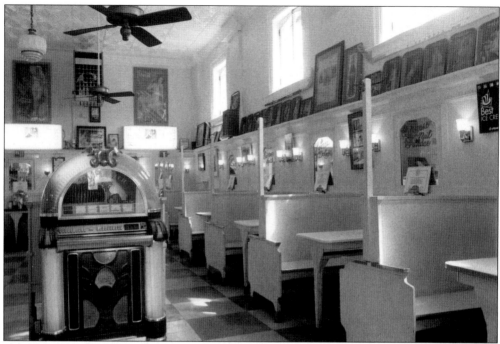

Dozens of old pictures adorn the top wall of the interior, which features popular booth seating as well.

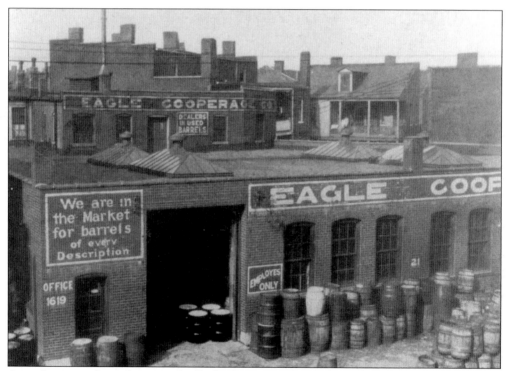

A productive industrial center, the Eagle Cooperage Co. is shown here during the early 20th century at 1619 Blair Avenue.

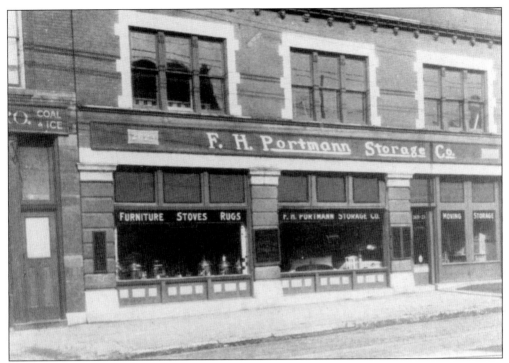

This respectable building at 2617–23 Cass Avenue houses the prosperous F.H. Portmann business. Photo *c.* 1920s.

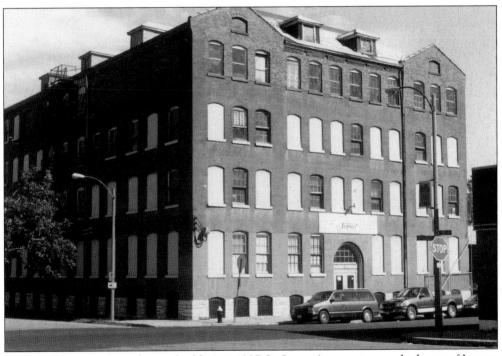

This long-time spaghetti factory building at 1227 St. Louis Avenue is now the home of Jayway Graphics, Inc.

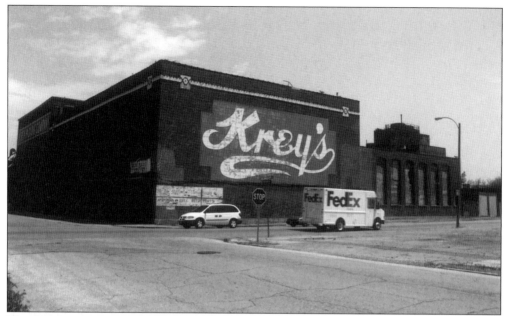

The famous meat company, Krey's, once occupied this building at N. Florissant and Bremen Avenues. It was built near the site of the old Hyde Park Brewery and stands near a cave where brew was stored. Until the 1920s, cattle were often herded here from the Union Stockyards near the Mississippi River.

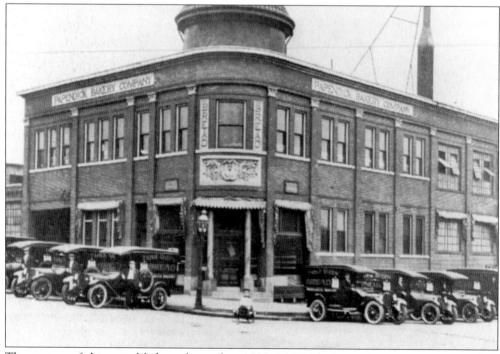

The owners of this noted bakery, located at 3500–16 N. Florissant Avenue, were reputed to have invented sliced bread. The business was going great guns in this picture of 1925. It was reported that the bakery turned out 30,000 loaves a day.

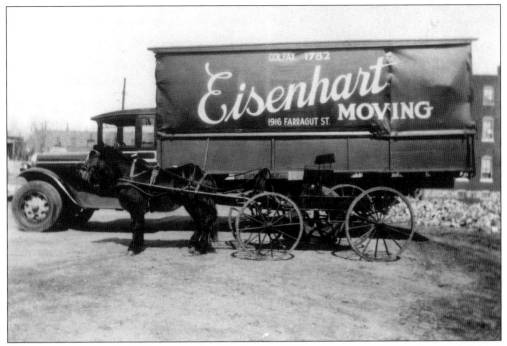

Here is a cameo study of the times: the Eisenhart vehicles.

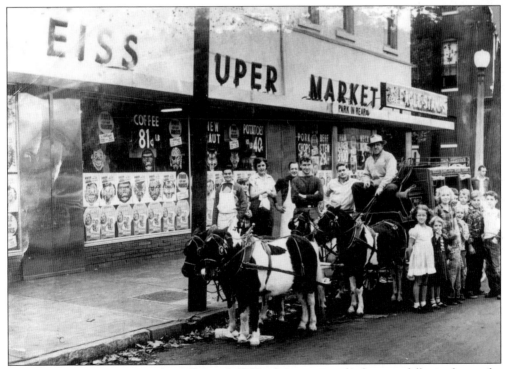

This attractive street scene from the mid-1950s shows a crowd of young folks in front of a supermarket at Broadway and Angelica Street. They are gathered around a stagecoach driven by a cowboy, who is handling the reins of a horse team.

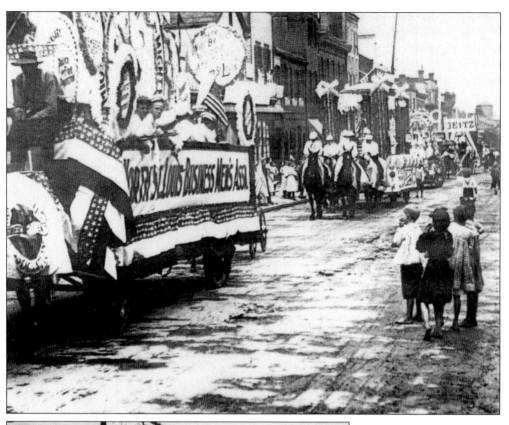

An indication that industry and business was flourishing at that time, the North St. Louis Business Association staged a parade on August 11, 1909.

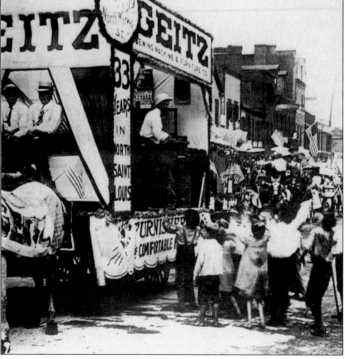

In that same parade, children receive treats from members of the Geitz float.

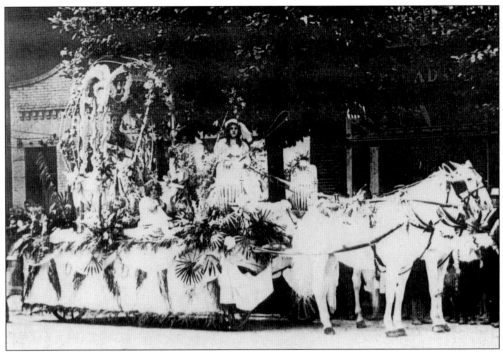

Another notable entry in the 1909 parade was this float called the "Flower Wagon of Adolf Brix."

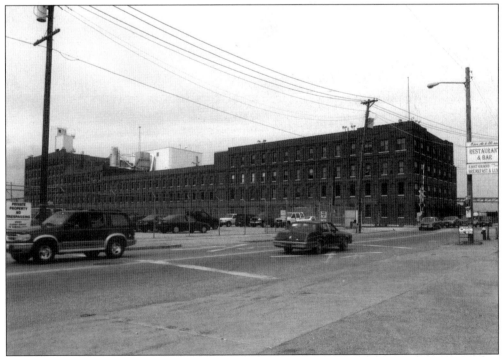

Here is a recent shot of a unit of the world-famous Procter and Gamble enterprise. It is located on E. Grand Avenue, close to the Mississippi River.

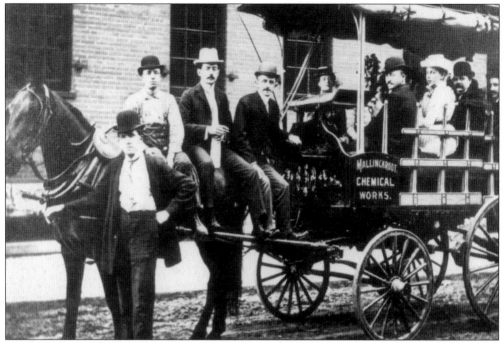

At the turn of the 20th century, a streetcar strike forced the Mallinckrodt Chemical Works to use a horse and wagon to transport workers.

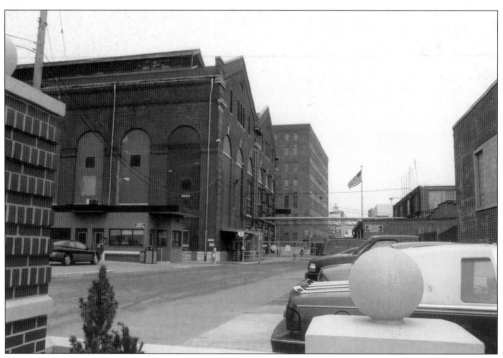

The Mallinckrodt firm was founded in 1867 in a one-room structure. It grew to be a giant in international business at Broadway and Mallinckrodt Street. Of great significance to WWII was the company's purification of the uranium used in the Manhattan Project.

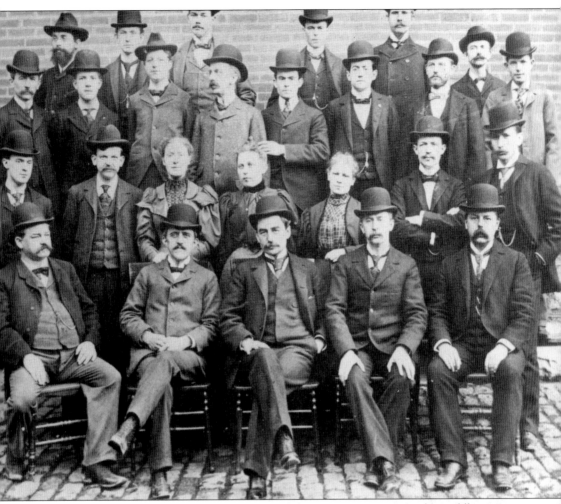

The employees of Mallinckrodt pose for this turn of the century portrait. At the middle center is Mallinckrodt himself.

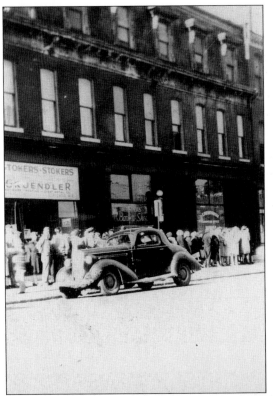

Just as St. Louis turned to Busch for beer, it turned to Piekutowski for sausage. This sausage became such a desirable item to so many people that the business has continued to the present day. In the early 1940s, lines of folk queued up to enter the shop. This was their first store, located at 1024 Cass Avenue.

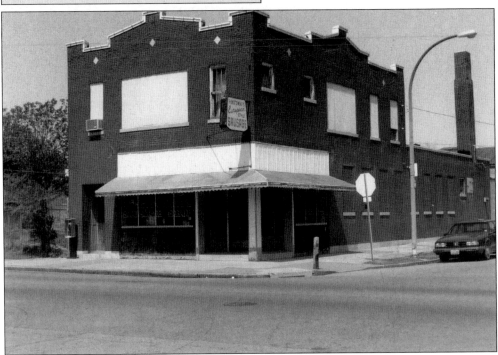

Pictured here is the business as it exists today. Piekutowski European Style Sausage has operated from 4100 N. Florissant Avenue since 1958.

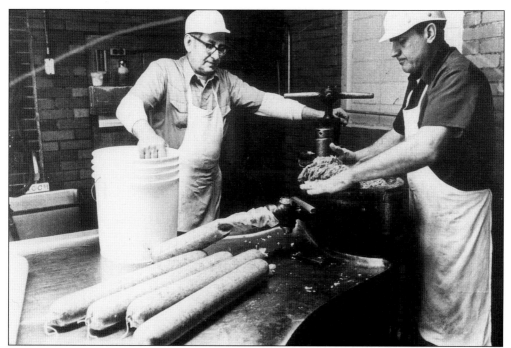

Two Piekutowski members prepare the sausage. The original owner, Ted, is on the left.

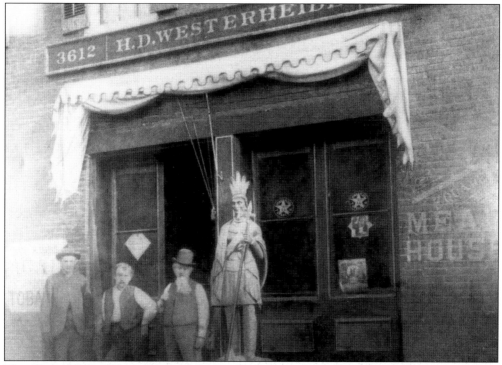

The Westerheide Tobacco and Cigar Company opened in 1860 and closed in early 2002. Pictured here in 1875 are the founder, his son (pictured at left), the last owners' grandfather, and great-grandfather. Since 1875 it was located at 3612 N. Broadway.

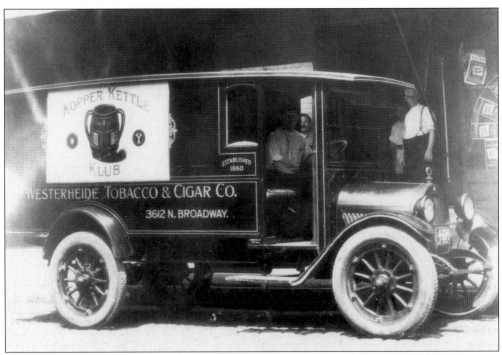

The firm promoted a private organization, the "Kopper Kettle Klub," as part of its advertising.

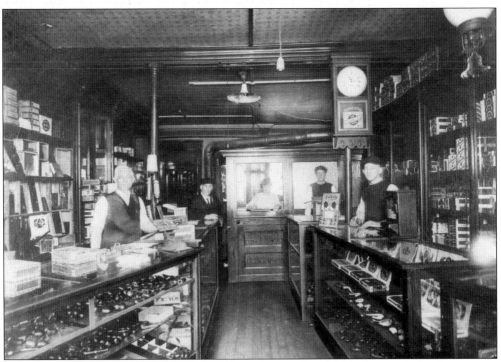

Another glance at the Westerheide firm in the 1920s shows its display room stocked with all variety of pipes and tobacco. A revered activity for centuries, pipe smoking draws aficionados to fine pipes and tobacco.

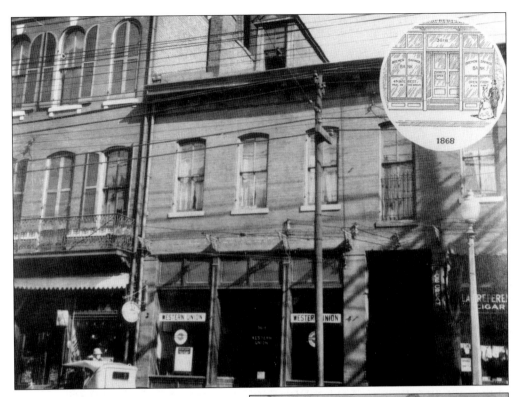

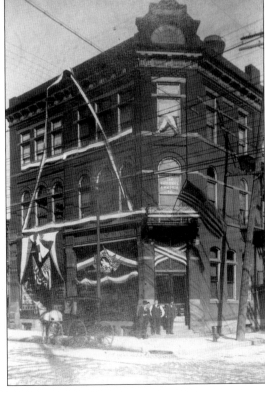

One of the most gracious and persistent promoters of North Side civic affairs is the Bremen Bank, currently located at Broadway and Mallinckrodt Street. It operated in three different locations. The first bank, pictured here in 1928, opened in 1868 and could be entered from a doorway directly from the sidewalk. It was active until 1888.

The second bank, activated in 1888, was the new home of the banking center.

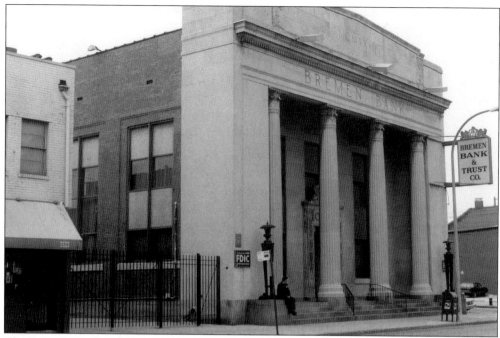

The Bremen Bank and Trust Company today is an impressive Greek-revival structure with 27-foot classical columns. The whole building is constructed of Bedford stone. Construction began in 1927.

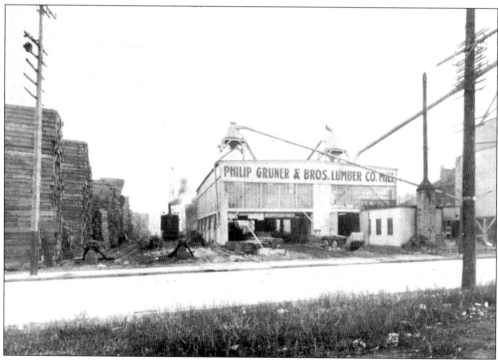

From the earliest days lumber was shipped down the Mississippi River to lumber yards on the north side. Photo *c.* 1920s.

Eleven

PLACES OF INTEREST

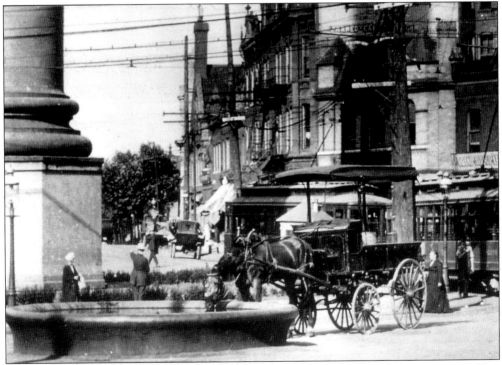

Of great interest to St. Louisans are the three splendid water towers that the city possesses. Two of these are in North St. Louis and the third near the reservoir at Grand and Lafayette Avenues in South St. Louis. Combining the utilitarian and the aesthetic, these extraordinary towers are an artistic success. This one is located at Grand Avenue and 12th Street, next to the watering trough for horses. (Photo courtesy of NPS.)

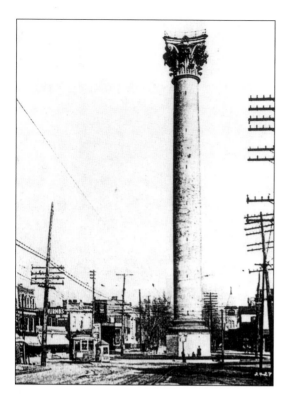

The water tower on Grand Avenue was the first to be built to help regulate the city's water demand. The city's first water works at Bissell Point needed a means of regulating the pressure of its output and thus these towers were built. Photo *c.* 1912.

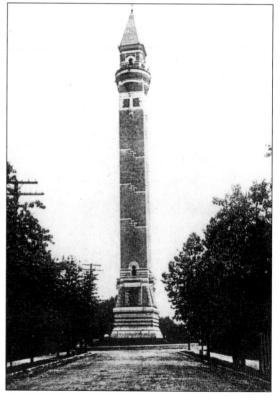

The second water tower was constructed of red-brick at Bissell Street. It was, at the time, the tallest in the city, rising to a height of almost 200 feet. Both towers were abandoned in the 20th century, but remain landmarks for the entire city. Photo *c.* 1912.

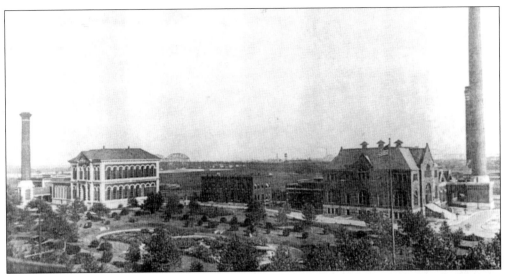

These high service pumping stations at Bissell Point operated as waterworks. The building on the left was erected in 1869.

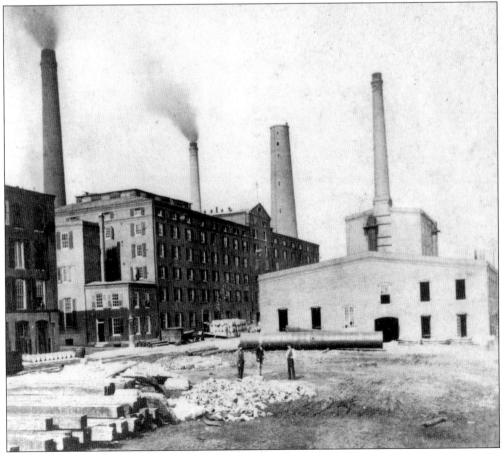

Pictured here are the main buildings of the waterworks at Bissell Point.

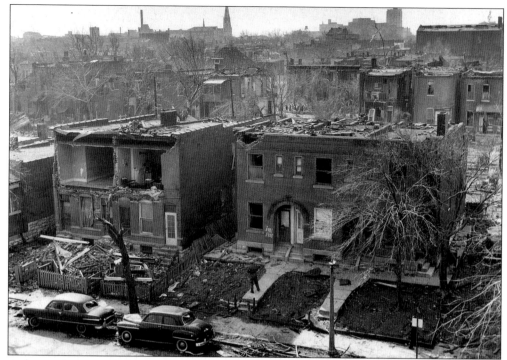

A destructive tornado hit St. Louis in 1959 and tore through areas of the Central West End, Gaslight Square, and parts of North St. Louis. Here is an image of the wrecked buildings, trees, and walls that were devoured by the ugly storm.

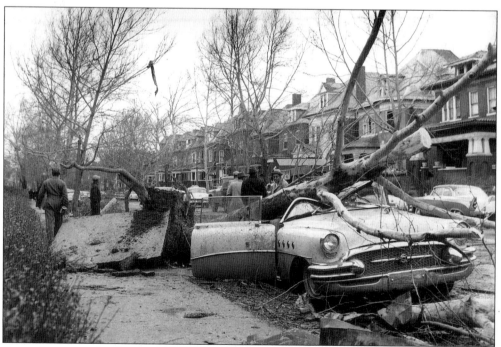

Bystanders assess the damage caused by the devastating tornado.

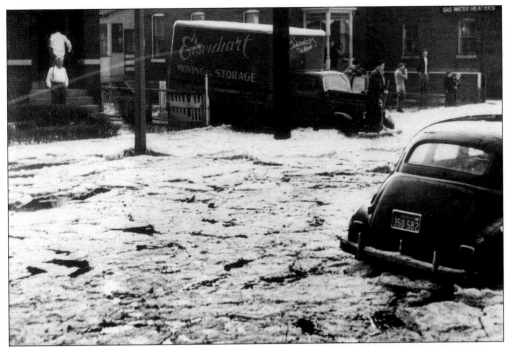

This photograph of an ice storm in early December 1950 is another example of the fierce storms that occasionally blow through St. Louis. This scene is on the 4200 block of 20th Street.

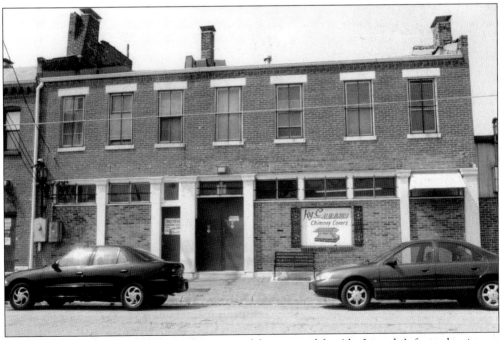

Some Civil War documents record that some of the material for Abe Lincoln's funeral train was purchased in St. Louis at J.H. Kobusch. The business occupied this building at 2109–13 North 14th Street. Now the sign on the building proclaims "HyC-Aluminum Chimney Covers."

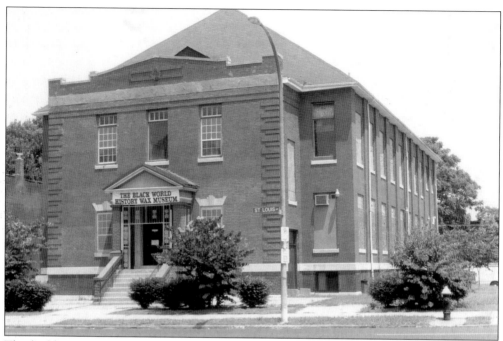

This building was once the school of the Most Sacred Heart Catholic Church. The church was demolished. Today, the building is home to The Black World History Wax Museum, which offers wax figures of prominent blacks and other exhibits related to black history.

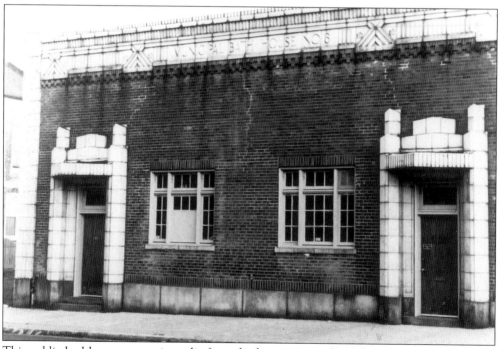

This public bathhouse, a genuine relic from the last century, charged 1¢ for towels and 1¢ for soap. These bathhouses were built at several locations throughout the city.

Twelve

RESTORATION

Various groups such as universities, churches, neighborhood associations, and individuals have sought to rejuvenate the Near North to bring it back to the condition of its vibrant early years. These supporters have bestowed grants, solicited foreign university students, inaugurated walking tours, founded church alliances, and organized street and ethnic festivals. The rehabbers, renovators, and restorers have all been busy hoping to contribute in large or small ways to the restoration of North St. Louis. Happily, progress is being made, to which the following pages attest, but a great deal has yet to be done. However, even slow progress promises what the whole city hopes for: a vital new life for North St. Louis.

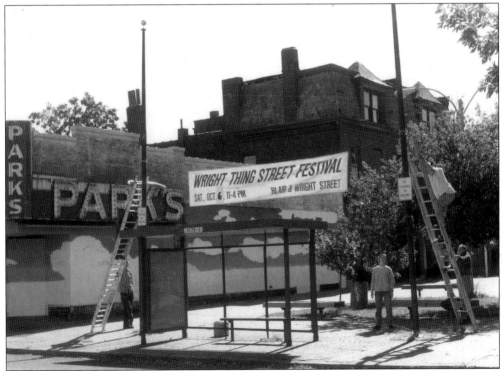

Pictured here is the Wright Thing Street Festival on the Near North Side.

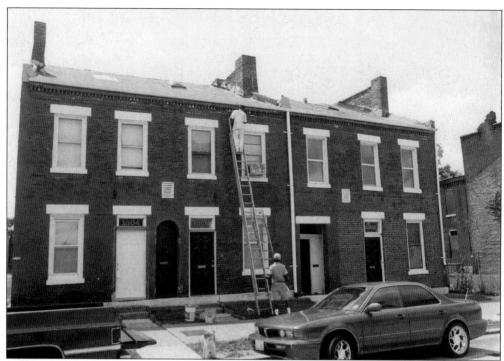

Collins and Collins is a firm devoted to rehabbing area houses. Pictured here on N. Market Street, two Collins' workmen rehabilitate another home.

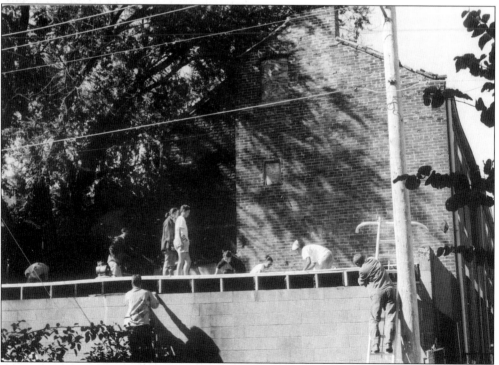

International students contribute to the renovation efforts at 1324 Wright Street.

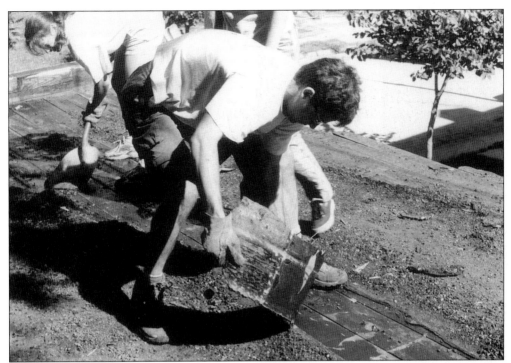

Lorene and Phillipe from France painstakingly tackle the old tar paper on the roof at 1324 Wright Street.

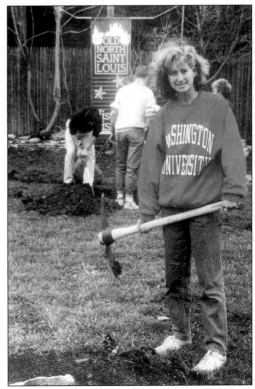

A young student wearing a Washington University shirt volunteers her time to help create a better neighborhood. Behind her waves a banner declaring that "heart work" is being done for the benefit of Old North St. Louis.

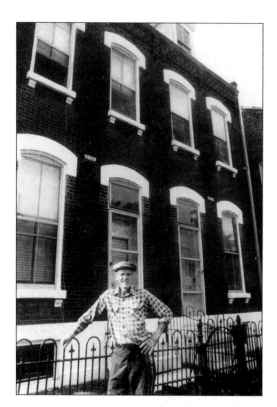

Ed Dueker faithfully maintains his building at Hebert Street and Blair Avenue.

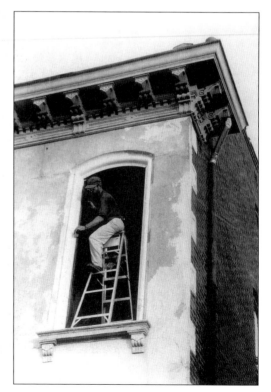

Tom Tschetter perches perilously on a ladder, working hard at his reconstruction effort.

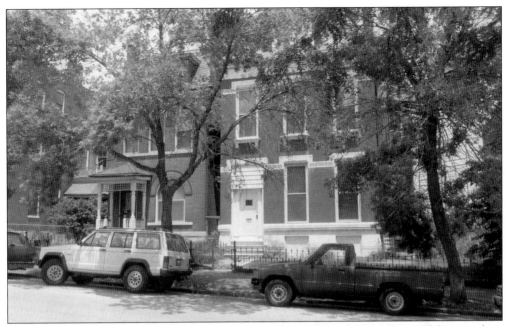

Tom and Gloria Bratkowski are tireless supporters of the North Side. Pictured here is their sparkling rehabilitation at 1209 Hebert Street. As various members of their family live close by, their domicile contributes to the closeness of their extended family.

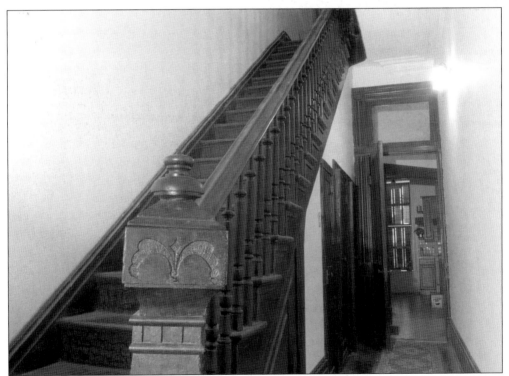

A handsome walnut banister graces their restored stairwell. This elegant staircase is headed by a giant newel post that adds authority and beauty.

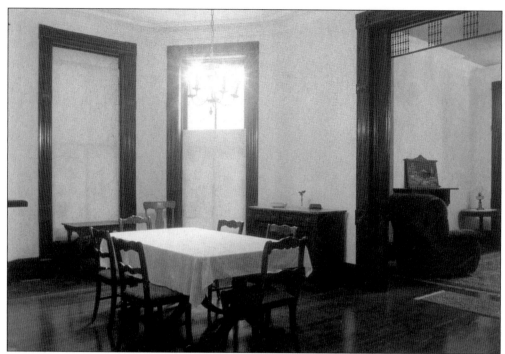

This dining room at 1209 Hebert Street is a classic. The sparse room, with simple, refinished floors, offers a pleasing aesthetic view.

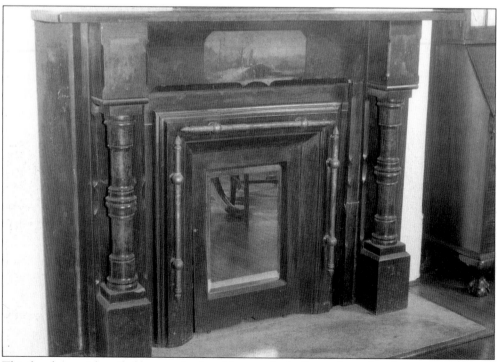

This fireplace, with a tiled base and painted images, is similar to those found in many Victorian homes.

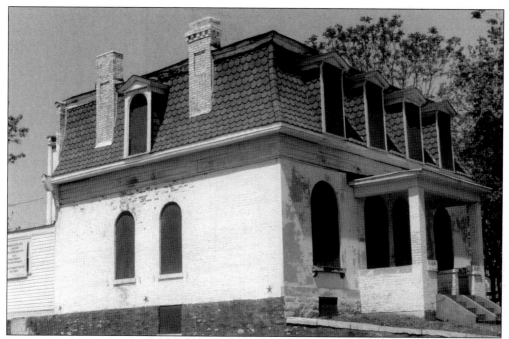

This 19th-century house at Blair and East Grand Avenues is noteworthy as it embodies certain fine Victorian features. The Missouri Department of Economic Development is partially underwriting a grant for the house's restoration.

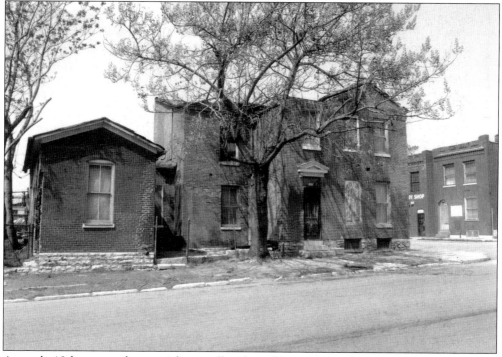

An early 19th-century house with a small utility addition, located at 2519 Blair Avenue, is a number of months away from complete restoration.

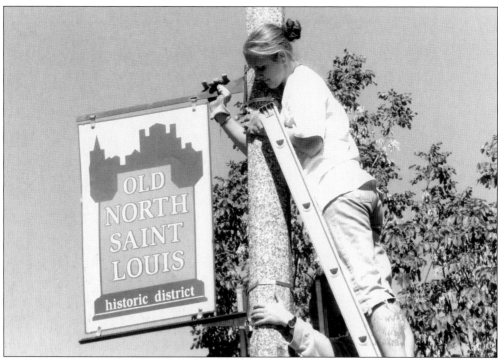

Hanna, a student from Germany, secures a banner that proclaims that she and her group are working to restore Old North St. Louis. Her efforts and the efforts of others depend on the continued support of those dedicated to creating a new North St. Louis. This can only be achieved with a coalition between government and community effort. This link will help foster the restoration of a historic and grand part of St. Louis.

Bibliography

A.B. Holcombe & Co. *Pitzman's New Atlas St. Louis, Missouri.* Philadelphia, Pennsylvania, 1878.

Compton, Richard J. and Camille N. Dry. *Pictorial St. Louis.* 1875

Fox, Tim, ed. *Where We Live: A Guide to St. Louis Communities.* Missouri Historical Society Press, 1995.

Hannon, Robert E., ed. *St. Louis: Its Neighborhood and Neighbors, Landmarks and Milestones.* St. Louis, Missouri. St. Louis Regional Commerce and Growth Association, 1986.

Old St. Louis and Yeatman History of St. Louis Neighborhoods. St. Louis Community Development Agency (Norbury L. Wayman), 1978.

Stiritz, Mary M. *St. Louis Historic Chuches and Synagogues.* St. Louis Public Library and Landmarks Association of St. Louis, Inc., 1995.

Who's Who in North St. Louis. North St. Louis Businessmen's Association, 1925.